Rules of the Senate of the United States, and Joint Rules of the Two Houses

1868, Oct. 1.

Hon. Chas. Sumner
(C. 6. 1830)

STANDING RULES

FOR

CONDUCTING BUSINESS

IN THE

SENATE OF THE UNITED STATES.

COMMENCEMENT OF DAILY SESSIONS.

1.——The Presiding Officer having taken the chair, and a quorum being present, the journal of the preceding day shall be read, to the end that any mistake may be corrected that shall be made in the entries.

[16 April, 1789—March 25, 1868.

A quorum shall consist of a majority of the Senators duly chosen and sworn.

[4 May, 1864—March 25, 1868.

BUSINESS NOT TO BE INTERRUPTED.

2.——No Senator shall speak to another, or otherwise interrupt the business of the Senate, or read any newspaper, while the journals or public papers are reading, or when any Senator is speaking in any debate.

[16 April, 1789—14 Feb., 1828—March 25, 1868.

RULES IN SPEAKING OR DEBATE.

3.——Every Senator, when he speaks, shall address the Chair, standing in his place, and when he has finished shall sit down.

[16 April, 1789—March 25, 1868.

4.——No Senator shall speak more than twice, in any one debate, on the same day, without leave of the Senate, which question shall be decided without debate.

[16 April, 1789—March 25, 1868.

5.——When two Senators rise at the same time, the Presiding Officer shall name the person to speak; but in all cases the Senator who shall rise first and address the Chair shall speak first.

[16 April, 1789—14 Feb., 1828—March 25, 1868.

CALLS TO ORDER AND APPEALS.

6.——If any Senator, in speaking or otherwise, transgress the rules of the Senate, the Presiding Officer shall, or any Senator may, call to order; and when a Senator shall be called to order by the Presiding Officer, or a Senator, he shall sit down, and shall not proceed without leave of the Senate. And every question of order shall be decided by the Presiding Officer, without debate, subject to an appeal to the Senate; and the Presiding Officer may call for the sense of the Senate on any question of order. But when an appeal shall be taken from the decision of the Presiding Officer, any subsequent question of order, which may arise before the decision of such appeal by the Senate, shall be decided by the Presiding Officer without debate, and every appeal therefrom shall also be decided at once, and without debate.

[16 April, 1789—14 Feb., 1828—26 June, 1856—March 25, 1868.

EXCEPTIONABLE WORDS.

7.——If a Senator be called to order by another for words spoken, the exceptionable words shall immediately be taken down in writing, that the Presiding Officer may be better able to judge of the matter.

[16 April, 1789—March 25, 1868.

ABSENT SENATORS MAY BE SENT FOR.

8.——No Senator shall absent himself from the service of the Senate, without leave of the Senate first obtained. And in case a less number than a quorum of the Senate shall convene, they are hereby authorized to send the Sergeant-at-arms, or any other person or persons by them authorized, for any or all absent Senators, as the majority of such Senators present shall agree, at the expense of such absent Senators, respectively, unless such excuse for non-attendance shall be made as the Senate, when a quorum is convened, shall judge sufficient, and in that case the expense shall be paid out of the contingent fund. And this rule shall apply as well to the first convention of the Senate, at the legal time of meeting, as to each day of the session, after the hour has arrived to which the Senate stood adjourned.

[16 April, 1789—25 June, 1798—4 Feb., 1828—March 25, 1868.

RULE FOR DEBATE.

9.——No motion shall be debated until the same shall be seconded.

[16 April, 1789—March 25, 1868.

RULE FOR MOTIONS, DEBATE, AND WITHDRAWAL.

10.——When a motion shall be made and seconded, it shall be reduced to writing, if desired by the Presiding Officer, or any Senator, delivered in at the table, and read, before the same shall be debated; and any motion may be withdrawn by the mover at any time before a decision, amendment, or ordering of the yeas and nays, except a motion to reconsider, which shall not be withdrawn without leave of the Senate.

[16 April, 1789—14 Feb., 1828—21 Jan., 1851—March 25, 1868.

11.——When a question is under debate, no motion shall be received but—

> to adjourn;
> to proceed to the consideration of Executive business;
> to lie on the table;
> to postpone indefinitely;
> to postpone to a day certain;
> to commit; or
> to amend ;

which several motions shall have precedence in the order they stand arranged; and motions to adjourn, to proceed to the consideration of Executive business, and to lie on the table, shall be decided without debate, and motions to take up or proceed to the consideration of any question shall be determined without debate upon the merits of the question proposed to be considered.

[16 April, 1789—13 Jan., 1820—14 Feb., 1828—March 25, 1868.

DIVISION OF A QUESTION.

12.——If the question in debate contain several points, any Senator may have the same divided; but, on a motion to strike out and insert, it shall not be in order to move for a division of the question; but the rejection of a motion to strike out and insert one proposition, shall not prevent a motion to strike out and insert a different proposition; nor prevent a subsequent motion simply to strike out; nor shall the rejection of a motion simply to strike out, prevent a subsequent motion to strike out and insert.

[16 April, 1789—23 June, 1832—March 25, 1868.

FILLING BLANKS.

13.——In filling up blanks, the largest sum and longest time shall be first put.

[16 April, 1789—3 Jan., 1820—14 Feb., 1828—March 25, 1868.

OBJECTION TO READING A PAPER.

14.——When the reading of a paper is called for, and the same is objected to by any Senator, it shall be determined by a vote of the Senate, and without debate.

[3 Jan., 1820—14 Feb., 1828—March 25, 1868.

UNFINISHED BUSINESS—PRIOR SPECIAL ORDER.

15.——The unfinished business in which the Senate was engaged at the last preceding adjournment shall have the preference in the special orders of the day.

[3 Jan., 1820—14 Feb., 1828—March 25, 1868.

YEAS AND NAYS.

16.——When the yeas and nays shall be called for by one-fifth of the Senators present, each Senator called upon shall, unless for special reasons he be excused by the Senate declare openly, and without debate, his assent or dissent to the question. In taking the yeas and nays, and upon a call of the Senate, the names of the Senators shall be called alphabetically.

[16 April, 1789—March 25, 1868.

17.——When the yeas and nays shall be taken upon any question, in pursuance of the above rule, no Senator shall be permitted, under any circumstances whatever, to vote after the decision is announced from the Chair.

[4 April, 1822—14 Feb., 1828—March 25, 1868.

CLOSING THE DOORS AND CLEARING THE GALLERY.

18.——On a motion made and seconded to shut the doors of the Senate, on the discussion of any business which may, in the opinion of a Senator, require secrecy, the Presiding Officer shall direct the gallery to be cleared; and during the discussion of such motion the doors shall remain shut.

[20 Feb., 1794—March 25, 1868.

NO PERSON ADMITTED TO PRESENT PETITION, ETC.

19.——No motion shall be deemed in order to admit any person whatsoever within the doors of the Senate Chamber to present any petition, memorial, or address, or to hear any such read.

[27 April, 1798—March 25, 1868.

RECONSIDERATION.

20.——When a question has been made and carried in the affirmative or negative, whether previously reconsidered or not, it shall be in order for any Senator of the majority to move for the reconsideration thereof; but no motion for the reconsideration of any vote shall be in order after the bill, resolution, message, report, amendment, or motion upon which the vote was taken shall have gone out of the possession of the Senate, announcing their decision, except a resolution confirming or rejecting a nomination by the President; nor shall any motion for reconsideration be in order, unless made on the same day on which the vote was taken, or within the two next days of actual session of the Senate thereafter; but a motion to reconsider a vote upon a nomination shall always, if the resolution announcing the decision of the Senate has been sent to the President, be accompanied by a motion requesting the President to return the same to the Senate. When any question may have been decided by the Senate, in which two-thirds of the Senators present are necessary to carry the affirmative, any Senator who votes on that side which prevailed in the question may be at liberty to move for a reconsideration; and a motion for reconsideration shall be decided by a majority of votes. But no motion to reconsider a vote upon a motion to reconsider shall be in order at any time.

[25 Feb., 1790—26 March, 1806—April 6, 1867—March 25, 1868.

CASTING VOTE OF THE VICE-PRESIDENT.

21.——When the Senate are equally divided, the President may announce his vote upon the question.

[18 July, 1789—March 25, 1868.

QUESTION PUT BY THE PRESIDING OFFICER.

22.——All questions shall be put by the Presiding Officer of the Senate, either in the presence or absence of the President of the United States, and the Senators shall signify their assent or dissent, by answering aye or no.

[21 Aug., 1789—March 25, 1868.

APPOINTMENT OF A SENATOR TO THE CHAIR.

23.——The Presiding Officer of the Senate shall have the right to name a Senator to perform the duties of the chair; but such substitution shall not extend beyond an adjournment.

[3 Jan., 1820—March 25, 1868.

MORNING BUSINESS, PETITIONS, REPORTS, ETC.

24.——After the journal is read, the Presiding Officer shall lay before the Senate messages from the President, reports from the Executive Departments, and bills and joint resolutions, or other messages from the House of Representatives. He shall then call for—

Petitions and memorials;

Reports of committees;

The introduction of bills;

Joint resolutions;

Resolutions;

all which shall be received and disposed of in such order, unless unanimous consent shall be otherwise given; and every petition or memorial, or other paper, shall be referred, of course, without putting a question for that purpose, unless the reference is objected to by a Senator at the time such petition, memorial, or other paper is presented. And before any petition or memorial, addressed to the Senate, shall be received and read at the table, whether the same shall be introduced by the Presiding Officer, or a Senator, a brief statement of the contents of the petition or memorial shall verbally be made by the introducer.

[18 April, 1789—10 April, 1834—March 25, 1868.

NOTICE AND PRINTING OF BILLS, ETC.

25.——One day's notice, at least, shall be given of an intended motion for leave to bring in a bill or joint resolution; and all bills and joint resolutions reported by a committee shall, after the first reading, be printed for the use of the Senate, and also all reports of committees. unless otherwise ordered; but no other paper or document shall be printed for the use of the Senate without special order.

[16 April, 1789—3 Feb., 1801—3 Jan., 1820—8 April, 1822—14 Feb., 1828—March 25, 1868.

JOINT RESOLUTIONS.

26.——Every bill and joint resolution shall receive three readings previous to its being passed, and the Presiding Officer shall give notice at each whether it be the first, second, or third; which reading shall be on three different days, unless the Senate unanimously direct otherwise. And all resolutions proposing amendments to the Constitution, or to which the approbation and signature of the President may be requisite, or which may grant money out of the contingent or any other fund, shall be treated, in all respects, in the introduction and form of proceeding on them, in the Senate, in a similar manner with bills; and all other resolutions shall lie on the table one day for consideration, and also reports of committees.

[March 25, 1868.

COMMITMENT OF BILLS.

27.——No bill or joint resolution shall be committed or amended until it shall have been twice read, after which it may be referred to a committee.

[16 April, 1789—March 25, 1868.

IN COMMITTEE OF THE WHOLE.

28.——All bills and joint resolutions on a second reading shall first be considered by the Senate in the same manner as if the Senate were in committee of the whole, before

they shall be taken up and proceeded on by the Senate agreeably to the standing rules, unless otherwise ordered.

[21 May, 1789—26 March, 1806—3 Jan., 1820—March 25, 1868.

FINAL QUESTIONS—REFERENCE TO COURT OF CLAIMS.

29.——The final question upon the second reading of every bill, resolution, or constitutional amendment, originating in the Senate; and requiring three readings previous to being passed, shall be, whether it shall be engrossed and read a third time; and no amendment shall be received for discussion at a third reading of any bill, resolution, or amendment, unless by unanimous consent of the Senators present; but it shall at all times be in order, before the final passage of any such bill, resolution, or constitutional amendment, to move its commitment; and should such commitment take place, and any amendment be reported by the committee, the said bill, resolution, or constitutional amendment, shall be again read a second time, and considered as in committee of the whole, and then the aforesaid question shall be again put. Whenever a private bill is under consideration, it shall be in order to move, as a substitute for it, a resolution of the Senate referring the case to the Court of Claims.

[4 Feb., 1807—26 June, 1856—March 25, 1868.

AMENDMENTS TO APPROPRIATION BILLS.

30.——No amendment proposing additional appropriations shall be received to any general appropriation bill, unless it be made to carry out the provisions of some existing law, or some act or resolution previously passed by the Senate during that session, or moved by direction of a standing or select committee of the Senate, or in pursuance of an estimate from the head of some of the departments; and no amendment shall be received whose object is to provide for a private claim, unless it be to carry out the provisions of an existing law or a treaty stipulation.

All amendments to general appropriation bills reported from committees of the Senate, proposing new items of appropriation, shall, one day before they are offered, be referred to the Committee on Appropriations, and all general appropriation bills shall be referred to the said committee.

[19 Dec., 1850—7 May, 1852—13 Jan., 1854—3 May, 1854—7 March, 1867—March 25, 1868.

SPECIAL ORDERS.

31.——When the hour shall arrive for the consideration of a special order, it shall be the duty of the Presiding Officer to take it up, unless the unfinished business of the preceding day shall be under consideration.

[26 June, 1856—March 25, 1868.

PRECEDENCE IN SPECIAL ORDERS.

When two or more subjects shall have been specially assigned for consideration, they shall take precedence according to the order of time at which they were severally assigned, and such order shall at no time be lost or changed except by the direction of the Senate.

[26 June, 1856—March 25, 1868.

PRECEDENCE IN SPECIAL ORDERS AND OVER GENERAL ORDERS.

When two or more subjects shall have been assigned for the same hour, the subject first assigned for that hour shall take precedence; but special orders shall always have precedence of general orders, unless such special orders shall be postponed by direction of the Senate.

[26 June, 1856—March 25, 1868.

TWO-THIRDS REQUIRED TO MAKE A SPECIAL ORDER.

No bill, joint resolution, or other subject, shall be made a special order for a particular day and hour without the concurrence of two-thirds of the Senators present.

[13 January, 1862—March 25, 1868

MAKING UP THE JOURNAL.

32.——The titles of bills and joint resolutions, and such parts thereof only as shall be affected by proposed amendments, shall be inserted on the journal.

[12 March, 1792—March 25, 1868.

33.——The proceedings of the Senate shall be entered on the journal as concisely as possible, care being taken to detail a true and accurate account of the proceedings; but every vote of the Senate shall be entered on the journal, and a brief statement of the contents of each petition, memorial, or paper, presented to the Senate, shall also be inserted on the journal.

[19 May, 1789—12 March, 1792—14 Feb., 1828—March 25, 1868.

STANDING COMMITTEES.

34.——The following standing committees shall be appointed at the commencement of each session, with leave to report by bill or otherwise:

[5 March, 1857—March 25, 1868.

A Committee on Foreign Relations, to consist of seven Senators.

[10 Dec., 1816—5 March, 1857—March 25, 1868.

A Committee on Finance, to consist of seven Senators.

[10 Dec., 1816—5 March, 1857—March 25, 1868.

A Committee on Appropriations, to consist of seven Senators.

[6 March, 1867—March 25, 1868.

A Committee on Commerce, to consist of seven Senators.

[10 Dec., 1816—7 Dec., 1825—5 March, 1857—March 25, 1868.

A Committee on Manufactures, to consist of five Senators.

[10 Feb., 1864—March 25, 1868.

A Committee on Agriculture, to consist of five Senators.

[6 March, 1863—March 25, 1868.

A Committee on Military Affairs, to consist of seven Senators.

[10 Dec., 1816—5 March, 1857—March 25, 1868.

A Committee on Naval Affairs, to consist of seven Senators.

[10 Dec., 1816—5 March, 1857—March 25, 1868.

A Committee on the Judiciary, to consist of seven Senators.

[10 Dec., 1816—5 March, 1857—March 25, 1868.

A Committee on Post Offices and Post Roads, to consist of seven Senators.

[10 Dec., 1816—5 March, 1857—March 25, 1868.

A Committee on Public Lands, to consist of seven Senators.

[10 Dec., 1816—5 March, 1857—March 25, 1868.

A Committee on Private Land Claims, to consist of five Senators.

[27 Dec., 1826—5 March, 1857—March 25, 1868.

A Committee on Indian Affairs, to consist of seven Senators.

[3 Jan., 1820—5 March, 1857—March 25, 1868.

A Committee on Pensions, to consist of seven Senators.

[10 Dec., 1816—5 March, 1857—March 25, 1868.

A Committee on Revolutionary Claims, to consist of five Senators.

[28 Dec., 1832—5 March, 1857—March 25, 1868.

A Committee on Claims, to consist of seven Senators.

[10 Dec., 1816—5 March, 1857—26 Jan., 1860—March 25, 1868.

A Committee on the District of Columbia, to consist of seven Senators.

[18 Dec., 1816—5 March, 1857—March 25, 1868.

A Committee on Patents, to consist of five Senators.

[7 Sept., 1837—5 March, 1857—March 25, 1868.

A Committee on Public Buildings and Grounds, to consist of five Senators, who shall have power also to act jointly with the same committee of the House of Representatives.

[16 Dec., 1819—19 Dec., 1837—28 May, 1850—5 March, 1857—March 25, 1868.

A Committee on Territories, to consist of seven Senators.

[25 March, 1844—5 March, 1857—March 25, 1868.

A Committee on the Pacific Railroad, to consist of nine Senators.

[22 Dec., 1863—March 25, 1868.

A Committee on Mines and Mining, to consist of seven Senators.

[8 March, 1865—March 25, 1868.

A Committee to Audit and Control the Contingent Expenses of the Senate, to consist of three Senators, to which shall be referred all resolutions directing the payment of money out of the contingent fund of the Senate, or creating a charge on the same.

[4 Nov., 1807—7 April, 1853—5 March, 1857—March 25, 1868.

A Committee on Printing, to consist of three Senators, to whom shall be referred every question on the printing of documents, reports, or other matter transmitted by either of the executive departments, and all memorials, petitions, accompanying documents, together with all other matter the printing of which shall be moved, excepting bills originating in Congress, resolutions offered by any Senator, communications from the Legislatures or Conventions lawfully called of the respective States, and motions to print by order of the standing committees of the Senate; motions to print additional numbers shall likewise be referred to said committee; and when the report shall be in favor of printing additional numbers, it shall be accompanied by an estimate of the probable cost; the said committee shall also supervise and direct the procuring of maps and drawings accompanying documents ordered to be printed.

[15 Dec., 1841—18 Dec., 1850—22 Jan., 1855—5 March, 1857—March 25, 1868.

A Committee on Engrossed Bills, to consist of three Senators, whose duty it shall be to examine all bills, amendments, and resolutions, before they go out of the possession of the Senate; and shall deliver the same to the Secretary of the Senate, who shall enter upon the journal that the same have been correctly engrossed.

[3 Jan., 1820—March 25, 1868.

A Committee on Enrolled Bills, to consist of three Senators, who, or some one of whom, shall forthwith present all enrolled Senate bills to the President in person, for his signature, and report the fact and date of such presentation to the Senate.

[6 Aug., 1789—5 March, 1857—March 25, 1868

APPOINTMENT OF COMMITTEES.

35.——In the appointment of the standing committees, the Senate will proceed, by ballot, to appoint severally the chairman of each committee, and then, by one ballot, the other members necessary to complete the same; and a majority of the whole number of votes given shall be necessary to the choice of a chairman of a standing committee, but a plurality of votes shall elect the other members thereof. All other committees shall be appointed by ballot, and a plurality of votes shall make a choice.

[3 Jan., 1820—8 Dec., 1826—14 Feb., 1828—March 25, 1868.

REFERENCE TO STANDING OR SELECT COMMITTEES

36.——When motions are made for reference of the same subject to a select committee and to a standing committee, the question on reference to the standing committee shall be first put.

[14 Feb., 1828—March 25, 1868.

EXECUTIVE BUSINESS—PROCEEDINGS ON NOMINATIONS.

37.——When nominations shall be made by the President of the United States to the Senate, they shall, unless otherwise ordered by the Senate, be referred to appropriate committees; and the final question on every nomination shall be, "Will the Senate advise and consent to this nomination?" which question shall not be put on the same day on which the nomination is received, nor on the day on which it may be reported by a committee, unless by the unanimous consent of the Senate. Nominations neither

approved nor rejected during the session at which they are made shall not be acted upon at any succeeding session without being again made by the President; and if the Senate shall adjourn or take a recess for more than thirty days, all nominations pending and not finally acted upon at the time of taking such adjournment or recess shall be returned to the President, and shall not be afterwards acted upon, unless again submitted to the Senate by the President; and all motions pending to reconsider a vote upon a nomination shall fall on such adjournment or recess; and the Secretary of the Senate shall thereupon make out and furnish to the heads of departments and other officers the list of nominations rejected or not confirmed, as required by law. When the President of the United States shall meet the Senate in the Senate Chamber for the consideration of executive business, the Presiding Officer of the Senate shall have a chair on the floor, be considered as the head of the Senate, and his chair shall be assigned to the President of the United States. When the Senate shall be convened by the President of the United States to any other place, the Presiding Officer of the Senate and the Senators shall attend at the place appointed, with the necessary officers of the Senate.

[21 Aug., 1789—18 Feb., 1843—March 25, 1868.

PROCEEDINGS ON TREATIES.

38.——When a treaty shall be laid before the Senate for ratification, it shall be read a first time, when no motion in respect to it shall be in order except to refer it to a committee or to print it in confidence for the use of the Senate. Its second reading shall be for consideration, and shall be on a subsequent day, when it shall be taken up as in Committee of the Whole and be considered by articles, when amendments may be proposed; but when amendments are reported by a committee they shall be first acted on, after which other amendments may be proposed; and when through, the whole proceedings had as in Committee of the

2

Whole shall be reported to the Senate, when the question shall be reported to the Senate, when the question shall be, if the treaty be amended, "Will the Senate concur in the amendments made in Committee of the Whole?" and the amendments may be taken separately or in gross, as the Senate may elect, after which new amendments may be proposed.   The decisions thus made shall be reduced to the form of a resolution of ratification, with or without amend-ments, as the case may be, which shall be proposed on a subsequent day, unless by unanimous consent the Senate determine otherwise, when every one shall again be free to move amendments, the question on which shall be proposed and taken as in the case of amendments to the article.   And on the final question to advise and consent to the ratifica-tion in the form agreed to, the concurrence of two-thirds of the Senators present shall be requisite to determine it in the affirmative, but all other motions and questions thereon shall be decided by a majority voto.

[6 Jan., 1801—March 25, 1868.

MATTERS CONFIDENTIAL AND SECRET.

39.——All confidential communications made by the President of the United States to the Senate shall be by the Senators and the Officers of the Senate kept secret, and all treaties which may be laid before the Senate, and all remarks and proceedings thereon, shall also be kept secret until the Senate shall, by their resolution, take off the injunction of secrecy.

[22 Dec., 1800—3 Jan., 1820—March 25, 1868.

SECRECY OF REMARKS ON NOMINATIONS.

40.——All information or remarks concerning the char-acter or qualifications of any person nominated by the President to office shall be kept a secret; but the fact that a nomination has been made shall not be regarded as a secret.

[3 Jan., 1820—March 25, 1868.

CLEARING OF THE SENATE.

41.——When acting on confidential or executive business, the Chamber shall be cleared of all persons except the secretary of the Senate, the principal or executive clerk, the sergeant-at-arms and doorkeeper, the assistant doorkeeper, and such other officers as the Presiding Officer shall think necessary; and all such officers shall be sworn to secrecy.

[3 Jan., 1820—March 25, 1868.

· SEPARATE BOOKS TO BE KEPT.

42.——The legislative proceedings, the executive proceedings, and the confidential legislative proceedings of the Senate, shall be kept in separate books.

[19 May, 1789—15 April, 1828—March 25, 1868.

EXECUTIVE PROCEEDINGS FURNISHED TO THE PRESIDENT.

43.——Nominations approved or definitely acted on by the Senate shall not be returned by the secretary of the Senate to the President until the expiration of the time limited for making a motion to reconsider the same, or while a motion to reconsider is pending, unless otherwise ordered by the Senate. The President of the United States shall, from time to time, be furnished with an authenticated transcript of the executive records of the Senate, but no further extract from the executive journal shall be furnished, except by special order; and no paper, except original treaties, transmitted to the Senate by the President of the United States, or any executive officer, shall be returned or delivered from the office of the secretary of the Senate, without an order of the Senate for that purpose.

[27 Jan., 1792—27 March, 1818—5 Jan., 1829—6 April, 1867—March 25, 1868.

PROCEEDINGS ON AMENDMENTS TO THE CONSTITUTION.

44.——When an amendment to be proposed to the Constitution is under consideration, the concurrence of two-

thirds of the Senators present shall not be requisite to decide any question for amendments, or extending to the merits, being short of the final question.

[26 March, 1806—March 25, 1868.

MESSAGES TO THE HOUSE OF REPRESENTATIVES.

45.——Messages shall be sent to the House of Representatives by the Secretary, who shall previously endorse the final determination of the Senate upon bills and other papers communicated.

[26 March, 1806—March 25, 1868.

MESSENGERS INTRODUCED.

46.——Messengers may be introduced in any state of business, except while a question is putting, while the yeas and nays are calling, or while the ballots are counting.

[26 March, 1806—March 25, 1868.

PERSONS ADMITTED ON FLOOR.

47.——No person shall be admitted to the floor of the Senate, while in session, except as follows, viz: The officers of the Senate, members of the House of Representatives and their clerk, the President of the United States and his private secretary, the heads of departments, ministers of the United States and foreign ministers, ex-Presidents and ex-Vice-Presidents of the United States, ex-Senators, Senators elect, judges of the Supreme Court, and Governors of States and Territories.

[17 March, 1853—23 Jan., 1854—24 Jan., 1854—6 March, 1856—11 Jan., 1859—7 Feb., 1862—March 25, 1868.

REGULATION OF SENATE WING OF THE CAPITOL.

48.——The Presiding Officer of the Senate shall have the regulation and control of such parts of the Capitol, and of its passages, as are or may be set apart for the use of the Senate and its officers.

[22 Jan., 1824—14 Feb., 1828—March 25, 1868.

RESTRICTION OF PRESENTING REJECTED CLAIMS.

49.——Whenever a claim is presented to the Senate and referred to a committee, and the committee report that the claim ought not to be allowed, and the report be adopted by the Senate, it shall not be in order to move to take the papers from the files for the purpose of referring them at a subsequent session, unless the claimant shall present a memorial for that purpose, stating in what respect the committee have erred in their report, or that new evidence has been discovered since the report, and setting forth the new evidence in the memorial.

[25 Jan., 1842—21 Dec., 1849—March 25, 1868.

PENALTIES FOR VIOLATING CONFIDENCE OF SENATE.

50.——Any Senator or officer of the Senate who shall disclose the secret or confidential business or ˙proceedings of the Senate shall be liable, if a Senator, to suffer expulsion from the body, and if an officer,· to dismissal from the service of the Senate, and to punishment for contempt.

[10 May, 1844—March 25, 1868.

OATHS OF OFFICE.

51.——The oaths or affirmations prescribed by the Constitution and by the act of Congress of July 2, 1862, to be taken and subscribed before entering upon the duties of office, shall be taken and subscribed by every Senator in open Senate before entering upon his duties. They shall also be taken and subscribed in the same way by the secretary of the Senate; but the other officers of the Senate may take and subscribe them in the office of the secretary.

[25 Jan., 1864—March 25, 1868.

BUSINESS CONTINUED FROM SESSION TO SESSION.

52.——At the second, or any subsequent, session of a Congress, the legislative business of the Senate which re-

mains undetermined at the close of the next preceding session of that Congress, shall be resumed and proceeded with in the same manner as if no adjournment of the Senate had taken place; and all subjects referred to committees, and not reported upon at the close of a session of Congress, shall be returned to the office of the secretary of the Senate, and be by him retained until the next succeeding session of that Congress, when they shall be returned to the several committees to which they had been previously referred.

[March 25, 1868.

SUSPENSION AND ADMENDMENT OF RULES.

53.——No motion to suspend, modify, or amend the rules, or any thereof, shall be in order, except on one day's notice in writing, specifying the rule to be suspended, modified, or amended, and the purpose thereof. But any rule may be suspended by unanimous consent, except the seventeenth rule, which shall never be suspended.

A motion to suspend, or to concur in a resolution of the House of Representatives to suspend, the 16th and 17th joint rules, or either of them, shall always be in order, be immediately considered, and be decided without debate.

[16 April, 1789—26 March, 1806—3 Jan., 1820—24 Feb., 1828—7 May, 1852—March 25, 1868.

RULES

OF

PROCEDURE AND PRACTICE IN THE SENATE,

WHEN SITTING ON THE

TRIAL OF IMPEACHMENTS,

AS

ADOPTED BY THE SENATE MARCH 2, 1868, AND AMENDED
MARCH 31, 1868, AND APRIL 3, 1868.

RULES

OF

PROCEDURE AND PRACTICE IN THE SENATE

WHEN SITTING ON THE TRIAL ON IMPEACHMENTS.

I. Whensoever the Senate shall receive notice from the House of Representatives that managers are appointed on their part to conduct an impeachment against any person, and are directed to carry articles of impeachment to the Senate, the Secretary of the Senate shall immediately inform the House of Representatives that the Senate is ready to receive the managers for the purpose of exhibiting such articles of impeachment agreeably to said notice.

II. When the managers of an impeachment shall be introduced at the bar of the Senate, and shall signify that they are ready to exhibit articles of impeachment against any person, the Presiding Officer of the Senate shall direct the Sergeant-at-arms to make proclamation, who shall, after making proclamation, repeat the following words, viz: "All persons are commanded to keep silence, on pain of imprisonment, while the House of Representatives is exhibiting to the Senate of the United States articles of impeachment against ——— ———;" after which the articles shall be exhibited, and then the Presiding Officer of the Senate shall inform the managers that the Senate will take proper order on the subject of the impeachment, of which due notice shall be given to the House of Representatives.

III. Upon such articles being presented to the Senate, the Senate shall, at one o'clock afternoon of the day (Sunday excepted) following such presentation, or sooner if so ordered

by the Senate, proceed to the consideration of such articles, and shall continue in session from day to day (Sundays excepted) after the trial shall commence, (unless otherwise ordered by the Senate,) until final judgment shall be rendered, and so much longer as may, in its judgment, be needful. Before proceeding to the consideration of the articles of impeachment, the Presiding Officer shall administer the oath hereinafter provided to the members of the Senate then present, and to the other members of the Senate as they shall appear, whose duty it shall be to take the same.

IV. When the President of the United States, or the Vice-President of the United States, upon whom the powers and duties of the office of President shall have devolved, shall be impeached, the Chief Justice of the Supreme Court of the United States shall preside; and in a case requiring the said Chief Justice to preside, notice shall be given to him by the Presiding Officer of the Senate of the time and place fixed for the consideration of the articles of impeachment, as aforesaid, with a request to attend; and the said Chief Justice shall preside over the Senate during the consideration of said articles, and upon the trial of the person impeached therein.

V. The Presiding Officer shall have power to make and issue, by himself or by the Secretary of the Senate, all orders, mandates, writs, and precepts authorized by these rules, or by the Senate, and to make and enforce such other regulations and orders in the premises as the Senate may authorize or provide.

VI. The Senate shall have power to compel the attendance of witnesses, to enforce obedience to its orders, mandates, writs, precepts, and judgments, to preserve order, and to punish in a summary way contempts of and disobedience to its authority, orders, mandates, writs, precepts, or judgments, and to make all lawful orders, rules, and regulations which it may deem essential or conducive to the

ends of justice. And the Sergeant-at-arms, under the direction of the Senate, may employ such aid and assistance as may be necessary to enforce, execute, and carry into effect the lawful orders, mandates, writs, and precepts of the Senate.

VII. The Presiding Officer of the Senate shall direct all necessary preparations in the Senate chamber, and the Presiding Officer on the trial shall direct all the forms of proceeding while the Senate are sitting for the purpose of trying an impeachment, and all forms during the trial not otherwise specially provided for. And the Presiding Officer on the trial may rule all questions of evidence and incidental questions, which ruling shall stand as the judgment of the Senate, unless some member of the Senate shall ask that a formal vote be taken thereon, in which case it shall be submitted to the Senate for decision; or he may at his option, in the first instance, submit any such question to a vote of the members of the Senate. Upon all such questions the vote shall be without a division, unless the yeas and nays be demanded by one-fifth of the members present when the same shall be taken.

VIII. Upon the presentation of articles of impeachment and the organization of the Senate as hereinbefore provided, a writ of summons shall issue to the accused, reciting said articles, and notifying him to appear before the Senate upon a day and at a place to be fixed by the Senate and named in such writ, and file his answer to said articles of impeachment, and to stand to and abide the orders and judgments of the Senate thereon; which writ shall be served by such officer or person as shall be named in the precept thereof, such number of days prior to the day fixed for such appearance as shall be named in such precept, either by the delivery of an attested copy thereof to the person accused, or if that cannot conveniently be done, by leaving such copy at the last known place of abode of such person, or at his

usual place of business in some conspicuous place therein; or if such service shall be, in the judgment of the Senate, impracticable, notice to the accused to appear shall be given in such other manner, by publication or otherwise, as shall be deemed just; and if the writ aforesaid shall fail of service in the manner aforesaid, the proceedings shall not thereby abate, but further service may be made in such manner as the Senate shall direct. If the accused, after service, shall fail to appear, either in person or by attorney, on the day so fixed therefor as aforesaid, or, appearing, shall fail to file his answer to such articles of impeachment, the trial shall proceed, nevertheless, as upon a plea of not guilty. If a plea of guilty shall be entered, judgment may be entered thereon without further proceedings.

IX. At twelve o'clock and thirty minutes afternoon of the day appointed for the return of the summons against the person impeached, the legislative and executive business of the Senate shall be suspended, and the Secretary of the Senate shall administer an oath to the returning officer in the form following, viz: "I, ——— ———, do solemnly swear that the return made by me upon the process issued on the ——— day of ———, by the Senate of the United States, against ——— ———, is truly made, and that I have performed such service as therein described: so help me God." Which oath shall be entered at large on the records.

X. The person impeached shall then be called to appear and answer the articles of impeachment against him. If he appear, or any person for him, the appearance shall be recorded, stating particularly if by himself, or by agent or attorney, naming the person appearing, and the capacity in which he appears. If he do not appear, either personally or by agent or attorney, the same shall be recorded.

XI. At twelve o'clock and thirty minutes afternoon of the day appointed for the trial of an impeachment, the legis-

lative and executive business of the Senate shall be suspended, and the Secretary shall give notice to the House of Representatives that the Senate is ready to proceed upon the impeachment of ——— ———, in the Senate chamber, which chamber is prepared with accommodations for the reception of the House of Representatives.

XII. The hour of the day at which the Senate shall sit upon the trial of an impeachment shall be (unless otherwise ordered) twelve o'clock m.; and when the hour for such sitting shall arrive, the Presiding Officer of the Senate shall so announce; and thereupon the Presiding Officer upon such trial shall cause proclamation to be made, and the business of the trial shall proceed. The adjournment of the Senate sitting in said trial shall not operate as an adjournment of the Senate; but on such adjournment, the Senate shall resume the consideration of its legislative and executive business.

XIII. The Secretary of the Senate shall record the proceedings in cases of impeachment as in the case of legislative proceedings, and the same shall be reported in the same manner as the legislative proceedings of the Senate.

XIV. Counsel for the parties shall be admitted to appear and be heard upon an impeachment.

XV. All motions made by the parties or their counsel shall be addressed to the Presiding Officer, and if he, or any Senator, shall require it, they shall be committed to writing, and read at the Secretary's table.

XVI. Witnesses shall be examined by one person on behalf of the party producing them, and then cross-examined by one person on the other side.

XVII. If a Senator is called as a witness, he shall be sworn, and give his testimony standing in his place.

XVIII. If a Senator wishes a question to be put to a witness, or to offer a motion or order, (except a motion to adjourn,) it shall be reduced to writing, and put by the Presiding Officer.

XIX. At all times while the Senate is sitting upon the trial of an impreachment the doors of the Senate shall be kept open, unless the Senate shall direct the doors to be closed while deliberating upon its decisions.

XX. All preliminary or interlocutory questions, and all motions, shall be argued for not exceeding one hour on each side, unless the Senate shall, by order, extend the time.

XXI. The case, on each side, shall be opened by one person. The final argument on the merits may be made by two persons on each side, (unless otherwise ordered by the Senate, upon application for that purpose,) and the argument shall be opened and closed on the part of the House of Representatives.

XXII. On the final question whether the impeachment is sustained, the yeas and nays shall be taken on each article of impeachment separately; and if the impeachment shall not, upon any of the articles presented, be sustained by the votes of two-thirds of the members present, a judgment of acquittal shall be entered; but if the person accused in such articles of impeachment shall be convicted upon any of said articles by the votes of two-thirds of the members present, the Senate shall proceed to pronounce judgment, and a certified copy of such judgment shall be deposited in the office of the Secretary of State.

XXIII. All the orders and decisions shall be made and had by yeas and nays, which shall be entered on the record, and without debate, subject, however, to the operation of Rule VII, except when the doors shall be closed for deliberation, and in that case no member shall speak more than once on one question, and for not more than ten minutes on an interlocutory question, and for not more than fifteen minutes on the final question, unless by consent of the Senate, to be had without debate; but a motion to adjourn may be decided without the yeas and nays, unless they be demanded by one-fifth of the members present.

XXIV. Witnesses shall be sworn in the following form, viz: "You, ——— ———, do swear (or affirm, as the case may be) that the evidence you shall give in the case now depending between the United States and ——— ———, shall be the truth, the whole truth, and nothing but the truth: so help you God." Which oath shall be administered by the Secretary, or any other duly authorized person.

Form of subpœna to be issued on the application of the managers of the impeachment, or of the party impeached, or of his counsel:

To ——— ———, greeting:

You and each of you are hereby commanded to appear before the Senate of the United States, on the ——— day of ———, at the Senate chamber in the city of Washington, then and there to testify your knowledge in the cause which is before the Senate in which the House of Representatives have impeached ——— ———.

Fail not.

Witness ——— ———, and Presiding Officer of the Senate, at the city of Washington, this ——— day of ———, in the year of our Lord ———, and of the independence of the United States the ———.

Form of direction for the service of said subpœna.

The Senate of the United States to ——— ———, greeting:

You are hereby commanded to serve and return the within subpœna according to law.

Dated at Washington, this ——— day of ———, in the year of our Lord ———, and of the independence of the United States the ———.

——— ———,
Secretary of the Senate.

Form of oath to be administered to the members of the Senate sitting in the trial of impeachments.

"I solemnly swear (or affirm, as the case may be) that in all things appertaining to the trial of the impeachment of ——— ———, now pending, I will do impartial justice according to the Constitution and laws: so help me God."

Form of summons to be issued and served upon the person impeached.

THE UNITED STATES OF AMERICA, *ss:*

The Senate of the United States to ——— ———, greeting:

Whereas the House of Representatives of the United States of America did, on the ——— day of ———, exhibit to the Senate articles of impeachment against you, the said ——— ———, in the words following:

[Here insert the articles.]

And demand that you, the said ——— ———, should be put to answer the accusations as set forth in said articles, and that such proceedings, examinations, trials, and judgments might be thereupon had as are agreeable to law and justice;

You, the said ——— ———, are therefore hereby summoned to be and appear before the Senate of the United States of America, at their chamber in the city of Washington, on the ——— day of ———, at twelve o'clock and thirty minutes afternoon, then and there to answer to the said articles of impeachment, and then and there to abide by, obey, and perform such orders, directions, and judgments as the Senate of the United States shall make in the premises according to the Constitution and laws of the United States.

Hereof you are not to fail.

Witness ——— ———, and Presiding Officer of the said Senate, at the city of Washington, this ——— day of ———, in the year of our Lord ———, and of the independence of of the United States the ———.

Form of precept to be endorsed on said writ of summons:

THE UNITED STATES OF AMERICA, *ss:*

The Senate of the United States to ——— ———, greeting:

You are hereby commanded to deliver to and leave with ——— ———, if conveniently to be found, or if not, to leave at his usual place of abode, or at his usual place of business in some conspicuous place, a true and attested copy of the within writ of summons, together with a like copy of this precept; and in whichsoever way you perform the service, let it be done at least ——— days before the appearance day mentioned in said writ of summons.

Fail not, and make return of this writ of summons and precept, with your proceedings thereon indorsed, on or before the appearance day mentioned in the said writ of summons.

Witness ——— ———, and Presiding Officer of the Senate, at the city of Washington, this ——— day of ———, in the year of our Lord ———, and of the independence of the United States the ———.

All process shall be served by the Sergeant-at-arms of the Senate, unless otherwise ordered by the court.

XXV. If the Senate shall at any time fail to sit for the consideration of articles of impeachment on the day or hour fixed therefor, the Senate may, by an order to be adopted without debate, fix a day and hour for resuming such consideration.

3

JOINT RULES

OF

THE TWO HOUSES.

JOINT RULES OF THE TWO HOUSES.

1.——In every case of an amendment of a bill agreed to in one House and dissented to in the other, if either House shall request a conference, and appoint a committee for that purpose, and the other House shall also appoint a committee to confer, such committee shall, at a convenient hour, to be agreed on by their chairmen, meet in the confer- ence chamber, and state to each other, verbally or in writing, as either shall choose, the reasons of their respective Houses for and against the amendment, and confer freely thereon.

[15 April, 1789.

MESSAGE SENT TO THE HOUSE OF REPRESENTATIVES.

2.——When a message shall be sent from the Senate to the House of Representatives, it shall be announced at the door of the House, by the Doorkeeper, and shall be re- spectfully communicated to the Chair by the person by whom it may be sent.

MESSAGE HOUSE OF REPRESENTATIVES TO SENATE.

3.——The same ceremony shall be observed when a message shall be sent from the House of Representatives to the Senate.

BY WHOM MESSAGES MAY BE SENT.

4.——Messages shall be sent by such persons as a sense of propriety in each House may determine to be proper.

ENGROSSED BILLS.

5.——While bills are on their passage between the two Houses, they shall be on paper, and under the signature of the Secretary or Clerk of each House, respectively.

[6 August, 1789.

ENROLLED BILLS.

6.——After a bill shall have passed both Houses, it shall be duly enrolled on parchment by the Clerk of the House of Representatives, or the Secretary of the Senate, as the bill may have originated in the one or the other House, before it shall be presented to the President of the United States.

[6 August, 1789.

EXAMINATION OF ENROLLED BILLS.

7.——When bills are enrolled they shall be examined by a joint committee of two from the Senate and two from the House of Representatives, appointed as a standing committee for that purpose, who shall carefully compare the enrollment with the engrossed bills, as passed in the two Houses, and, correcting any errors that may be discovered in the enrolled bills, make their report forthwith to their respective Houses.

[6 August, 1789—1 Feb., 1827.

SIGNING OF ENROLLED BILLS.

8.——After examination and report, each bill shall be signed in the respective Houses, first by the Speaker of the House of Representatives, then by the President of the Senate.

[6 August, 1789.

PRESENTATION OF ENROLLED BILLS TO THE PRESIDENT.

9.——After a bill shall have been thus signed in each House, it shall be presented by the said committee to the

President of the United States, for his approbation, (it being first endorsed on the back of the roll, certifying in which House the same originated; which endorsement shall be signed by the Secretary or Clerk, as the case may be, of the House in which the same did originate,) and shall be entered on the journal of each House. The said committee shall report the day of presentation to the President; which time shall also be carefully entered on the journal of each House.

[6 August, 1789.

SAME PROCEEDINGS AS ABOVE ON ORDERS, RESOLUTIONS, AND VOTES, AS ON BILLS.

10.——All orders, resolutions, and votes, which are to be presented to the President of the United States for his approbation, shall also, in the same manner, be previously enrolled, examined and signed; and shall be presented in the same manner, and by the same committee, as provided in the cases of bills.

[6 August, 1789.

JOINT ADDRESS TO THE PRESIDENT.

11.——When the Senate and House of Representatives shall judge it proper to make a joint address to the President, it shall be presented to him in his audience chamber by the President of the Senate, in the presence of the Speaker and both Houses.

[6 August, 1789.

NOTICE OF REJECTED BILL.

12.——When a bill or resolution which shall have passed in one House is rejected in the other, notice thereof shall be given to the House in which the same shall have passed.

10 August, 1790.

REJECTED BILL NOT RENEWED WITHOUT TEN DAYS' NOTICE.

13.——When a bill or resolution which has been passed in one House shall be rejected in the other, it shall not be brought in during the same session, without a notice of ten days and leave of two-thirds of·that House in which it shall be renewed.

[10 June, 1790.

PAPERS TO BE SENT WITH BILLS.

14.——Each House shall transmit to the other all papers on which any bill·or resolution shall be founded.

[10 June, 1790.

ADHERENCE BY EACH HOUSE DESTROYS BILL.

15.——After each House shall have adhered to their disagreement, a bill or resolution shall be lost.

[10 June, 1790.

BILL NOT TO BE SENT TO OTHER HOUSE ON THREE LAST DAYS OF SESSION.

*16.——No bill that shall have passed one House shall be sent for concurrence to the other on either of the last three days of the session.

BILL NOT TO BE SENT TO THE PRESIDENT ON LAST DAY OF SESSION.

*17.——No bill or resolution that shall have passed the House of Representatives and the Senate shall be presented to the President of the United States, for his approbation, on the last day of the session.

* By the 26th Rule of the Senate: A motion to suspend or concur in resolution of H. R. to suspend the 16th and 17th Joint Rules, or either of them, shall always be in order, immediately considered, and decided without debate.

[7 May, 1852.

PRINTING OF BILLS BY THE OTHER HOUSE.

18. ——When bills which have passed one House are ordered to be printed in the other, a greater number of copies shall not be printed than may be necessary for the use of the House making the order.

[9 Feb., 1829.

SALE OF INTOXICATING LIQUORS FORBIDDEN.

19. ——No spirituous or malt liquors or wines shall be offered for sale, exhibited, or kept within the Capitol, or in any room or building connected therewith, or on the public grounds adjacent thereto. And it shall be the duty of the Sergeants-at-arms of the two Houses, under the supervision of the presiding officers thereof, respectively, to enforce the foregoing provisions. And any officer or employé of either House who shall in any manner violate, or connive at the violation of this rule shall be dismissed from office.

[18 Sept., 1837—H. R., 26 Feb., 1844—S., 30 May, 1844.

JOINT COMMITTEE ON THE LIBRARY.

20. ——There shall be a joint committee on the Library, to consist of three members on the part of the Senate and three on the part of the House of Representatives, to superintend and direct the expenditure of all moneys appropriated for the Library, and to perform such other duties as are or may be directed by law.

[S., 6 Dec., 1843—H. R., 7 Dec., 1843.

CONTINUANCE OF BUSINESS AT SUBSEQUENT SESSION.

21. ——After six days from the commencement of a second or subsequent session of Congress, all bills, resolutions, or reports, which originated in either House, and at the close of the next preceding session remained undetermined in either House, shall be resumed and acted on in the same manner as if an adjournment had not taken place.

[14 August, 1848.

22.——The two Houses shall assemble in the hall of
the House of Representatives at the hour of one o'clock p.
m., on the second Wednesday in February next succeeding
the meeting of the electors of President and Vice-President
of the United States, and the President of the Senate shall
be their presiding officer; one teller shall be appointed on
the part of the Senate and two on the part of the House of
Representatives, to whom shall be handed, as they are
opened by the President of the Senate, the certificates of
the electoral votes; and said tellers, having read the same
in the presence and hearing of the two Houses then assembled, shall make a list of the votes as they shall appear from
the said certificates; and the votes having been counted, the
result of the same shall be delivered to the President of the
Senate, who shall thereupon announce the state of the vote
and the names of the persons, if any, elected; which an-
nouncement shall be deemed a sufficient declaration of the
persons elected President and Vice-President of the United
States, and, together with a list of the votes, be entered on
the journals of the two Houses.   If, upon the reading of any
such certificate by the tellers, any question shall arise in regard to counting the votes therein certified, the same having
been stated by the Presiding Officer, the Senate shall thereupon withdraw, and said question shall be submitted to that
body for its decision; and the Speaker of the House of Representatives shall, in like manner, submit said question to the
House of Representatives for its decision; and no question
shall be decided affirmatively, and no vote objected to shall
be counted, except by the concurrent votes of the two
Houses; which being obtained, the two Houses shall immediately reassemble, and the Presiding Officer shall then announce the decision of the question submitted, and upon
any such question there shall be no debate in either House;
and any other question pertinent to the object for which
the two Houses are assembled may be submitted and deter-

mined in like manner. At such joint meeting of the two Houses seats shall be provided as follows: for the President of the Senate, the "Speaker's chair," for the Speaker, a chair immediately upon his left; the Senators in the body of the hall, upon the right of the Presiding Officer; for the representatives, in the body of the hall not occupied by the Senators; for the tellers, Secretary of the Senate, and Clerk of the House of Representatives, at the Clerk's desk; for the other officers of the two Houses, in front of the Clerk's desk and upon either side of the Speaker's platform. Such joint meeting shall not be dissolved until the electoral votes are all counted and the result declared; and no recess shall be taken unless a question shall have arisen in regard to counting any of such votes, in which case it shall be competent for either House, acting separately, in the manner hereinbefore provided, to direct a recess, not beyond the next day at the hour of one o'clock p. m.

ANALYTICAL INDEX

TO THE

RULES OF THE SENATE.

A.

No.

ABSENT himself from Senate, without leave first obtained. No member
shall 8

ABSENT members may be sent for, by less than a quorum, at the expense
of such members, unless excused, and then paid out of the contingent
fund.. 8

ADDITIONAL numbers of documents to be referred to the Committee on
Printing. Motions to print................................. 34

ADDRESS, or hear any such read. No person shall be admitted to present
any petition, memorial, or................................. 19

ADJOURN, &c. When a question is under debate, no motion shall be
received but to.. 11

ADJOURNMENT shall always be in order, and shall be decided without
debate. The motion for.................................... 11

ADJOURNMENT. The substitution of a member to fill the chair shall not
extend beyond an.. 23

ADJOURNMENTS. Special orders not to lose their position on the calendar
on account of intervening................................. 31

ADMIT any person in Senate to present a petition, &c., &c. No motion in
order to... 19

ADMITTED on the floor of the Senate. Description of persons (and none
others) who shall be...................................... 47

AGRICULTURE, to consist of five members. A standing Committee on.... 34

ALPHABETICALLY. In taking the yeas and nays, or on a call of the House,
the names of the members taken............................ 16

AMEND. When a question is under debate, no motion shall be received
but to adjourn, to lie on the table, to postpone indefinitely, to postpone
to a day certain, to commit, or to......................... 11

AMENDED until twice read, &c. No bill shall be..................... 27

AMENDMENT. Any motion may be withdrawn before.................. 10

AMENDMENTS containing several points may be divided, but a motion to
strike out and insert shall not be divided. The rejection of a motion
to strike out and insert one proposition shall not prevent a motion to
strike out and insert a different proposition, nor a motion simply to
strike out, nor another motion to strike out and insert.... 2

No.

AMEND the rules. One day's notice of a motion required to............. 53
AMENDMENTS to the Constitution same as on bills, &c. The proceedings
on...................... 26
AMENDMENT. No amendment shall be received for discussion at a third
reading of any bill, &c., unless by unanimous consent; but such bill,
&c., may be referred to a committee, and should an amendment be
reported, the bill, &c., shall again be read a second time, &c., (see
Rule).. 29
AMENDMENT shall be, "Whether it shall be engrossed and read a third
time?" The final question on the second reading of any constitutional 29
AMENDMENT proposing additional appropriations shall not be received to
any general appropriation bill, unless to carry out an existing law, or
act, or resolution of the Senate previously passed during that session,
or moved by a standing or select committee, or in pursuance of an
estimate from the head of some of the departments; and no amendment shall be received to provide for a private claim, unless it be to
carry out an existing law or treaty stipulation...................... 30
AMENDMENTS to general appropriation bills, proposing new items of appropriation, shall, one day before they are offered, be referred to the
Committee on Appropriations....................................... 30
AMENDMENTS shall be inserted on the journals. The titles of bills and
parts affected by... 32
AMENDMENTS to treaties. Forms of questions and proceedings on....... 38
AMENDMENT to be proposed to the Constitution is under-consideration, the
concurrence of two-thirds of the members present shall not be requisite
to decide any question for amendments, or extending to the merits, being
short of the final question. When an............................... 44
APPEAL to the Senate. Every question of order shall be decided by the
President, without debate, subject to an............................ 6
APPOINTMENT of all the committees (except the chairman of standing
committees) a plurality of votes shall make a choice. In the........ 35
APPOINTMENT of standing committees the Senate will proceed, by ballot,
severally to appoint the chairman of each committee, and then, by one
ballot, the other members necessary to complete the same; and a
majority of the whole number of votes given shall be necessary to the
choice of a chairman of a standing committee. All other committees
shall be appointed by ballot, and a plurality of votes shall make a
choice. In the.. 35
APPOINTMENTS. Executive, &c. (See Nominations.)
APPROPRIATION bill. Restrictions upon amendments to any general (see
Amendment—Rule—Bill)... 30
APPROPRIATIONS to consist of seven members. A standing committee on.. 34
ASSIGNMENT of special orders according to the order of time for which
they were assigned, and at which they were assigned, and over general
orders ....:.............................. 31
ATTENDANCE of members required and absent members sent for, &c...... 8

No.

AUDIT and Control the Contingent Expenses of the Senate, to consist of three members, to whom shall be referred all resolutions directing the payment of money out of the contingent fund of the Senate, or creating a charge on the same. Standing Committee to...................... 34
AYE or No. The President of the Senate shall put all questions, and the members shall answer... 22

B.

BALLOT, &c. All standing and other committees shall be appointed by.. 35
BALLOTS are being counted, &c. Messengers are introduced in any state of business, except while the... 46
BILL, resolution, &c., has gone out of possession of the Senate. No motion for reconsideration shall be in order after a......................... 20
BILL. One day's notice shall be given for asking leave to introduce a.... 25
BILLS reported by a committee shall, after first reading, be printed....... 25
BILL shall receive three readings before being passed. Each............. 20
BILL, which readings shall be on different days, unless Senate unanimously direct otherwise. The President shall give notice at *first*, *second*, and *third* reading of each... 26
BILLS. All resolutions requiring the signature of the President, or granting money out of contingent or other fund, shall be treated as............. 26
BILL shall be committed or amended until it shall have been twice read, after which it may be committed. No............................... 27
BILLS on a second reading shall first be considered as in Committee of the Whole before being considered in Senate, unless otherwise ordered. All... 28
BILL in Committee of the Whole, the Vice-President, or President *pro tempore*, may call a member to fill the chair, &c. When the Senate shall consider a.. 28
BILL originating in the Senate shall be, "Whether it shall be engrossed and read a third time?" The final question on the second reading of every... 29
BILL, unless by unanimous consent of the members present. No amendment shall be received for discussion at the third reading of any........... 29
BILL, to move its commitment. It shall at all times be in order, before the final passage of any... 29
BILLS reported with any amendment, after such commitment, shall be again read a second time and considered as in Committee of the Whole, and then the question shall again be put, "Whether it shall be engrossed and read a third time?"... 29
BILL is under consideration, it shall be in order to move, as a substitute for it, a resolution of the Senate referring the case to the Court of Claims. Whenever a private.. 29
BILL, unless to carry out the provisions of some existing law, or act, or resolution previously passed by the Senate, during that session, or moved by direction of a standing or select committee of the Senate, or

No.

in pursuance of an estimate from the head of some of the departments; and no amendment shall be received whose object is to provide for a private claim, unless it be to carry out the provisions of an existing law or a treaty stipulation. No amendment proposing additional appropriations shall be received to any general appropriation 30

BILLS and such parts only as shall be affected by proposed amendments shall be inserted on the journals. The titles of 32

BILL or otherwise. The standing committees of the Senate shall be appointed at the commencement of each session, with leave to report by .. 34

BILLS, to consist of three members, whose duty it shall be to examine all bills, &c., before they go out of the possession of the Senate, and deliver same to Secretary of the Senate, to be entered on the journal as correctly engrossed. A Committee on Engrossed 34

BILLS to be printed without being referred to the Committee on Printing .. 34

BILLS, to consist of three members. A Committtee on Enrolled 34

BLANKS the largest sum and longest time shall be first put. In filling 13

BOOKS (or journals.) The legislative proceedings, the executive proceedings, and the confidential legislative proceedings of the Senate, shall be kept in separate and distinct 42

BUSINESS of Senate not to be interrupted by talking, reading newspapers, or otherwise 2

BUSINESS at preceding adjournment shall have preference in the *special orders* of the day. The unfinished 15

BUSINESS requiring secrecy the doors shall be shut, &c. On the discussion of 18

BUSINESS in the Senate. Order of morning 24

BUSINESS except while a question is being put, while the yeas and nays are being called, or while the ballots are being counted. Messengers are introduced in any state of the 46

BUSINESS to be continued from session to session of a Congress 52

C.

CALENDAR on account of intervening adjournments. Special orders not to lose their position on the 31

CALL of the House, the names taken alphabetically. Upon a 16

CAPITOL, and of its passages, as are or may be set apart for the use of the Senate and its officers. The Presiding Officer of the Senate shall have the regulation of such parts of the 48

CASTING vote. When the Senate are equally divided the President shall give the 21

CHAIR, and, a quorum being present, the business proceeds. The President takes the 1

CHAIR. Every member, when he speaks, shall address the 3

CHAIR. Every member, rising to speak, shall address the 3

CHAIR shall speak first, the Chair to name the member. The member who shall first rise and address the 5

No.

CHAIR shall, or a member may, call to order when rules are transgressed. The 6

CHAIR no member shall be permitted to vote. When the decision shall be announced by the 17

CHAIR, but such substitution shall not extend beyond an adjournment. The Vice-President, or President *pro tempore*, shall have the right to name a member to perform the duties of the 23

CHAIR during the time the Senate shall remain in Committee of the Whole; and the chairman so called shall, during such time, have the powers of a President *pro tempore*. When the Senate shall consider a treaty, bill, or resolution, as in Committee of the Whole, the Vice-President, or President *pro tempore*, may call a member to fill the 28

CHAIR to take up such special order, and it shall be considered unless postponed by a vote of the Senate. When the hour has arrived for the consideration of a special order, it shall be the duty of the 31

CHAIRMAN of the Committee of the Whole shall, during the time of remaining in such committee, have the powers of a President *pro tempore*. The 28

CHAIRMAN of each standing committee, the Senate shall proceed by ballot, and a majority of the whole number of votes given shall be necessary to a choice. In the appointment of the 35

CHARACTER or qualification of any person nominated by the President to office shall be kept secret. All information or remarks touching or concerning the 40

CLAIMS in appropriation bills. Restrictions upon amendments providing for private 30

CLAIMS, to consist of five members. A standing Committee on 34

CLAIMS reported against and rejected. Restriction on the presentation of.. 49

CLAIM is presented to the Senate and referred to a committee, and the committee report that the claim ought not to be allowed, and the report be adopted by the Senate, it shall not be in order to move to take the papers from the files for the purpose of referring them at subsequent sessions, unless the claimants shall present a memorial for that purpose, stating in what manner the committee have erred in their report, or that new evidence has been discovered since the report, and setting forth the new evidence in the memorial: *Provided*, That this rule shall not extend to any case where an adverse report, not in writing, shall have been made prior to January 25, 1842. Whenever a 49

COMMERCE, to consist of seven members. A standing Committee on. 34

COMMITTEES of the Senate. Appointment of, (see *Standing Committees—see Rule*) 34

COMMITTEES. (See *Reports* of.)

COMMITTEES, (except the chairman of standing committees, who shall be appointed by a majority,) a plurality of votes shall make a choice. In the appointment by ballot of all of the........................... 35

4

No.

COMMITTEE shall first be put. When motions are made for reference of the same subject to a select committee, and to a standing committee, the question on reference to the standing 36

COMMITTEE, any other subject or matter of a similar nature may, on motion, be referred to such committee. When any subject or matter shall have been referred to a 35

COMMITTED or amended until twice read, after which it may be referred to a committee. No bill shall be................. 27

COMMITTEE to be printed after first reading. All bills reported by a..... 25

COMMITTEES to be called for in morning business after petitions, &c. Reports of standing.. 24

COMMIT or to amend, &c., &c. When a question is under debate, no motion shall be received but to adjourn or to............................. 11

COMMITTEE have erred in their report, or that new evidence has been discovered. Not in order to move to refer a claim which has been reported upon adversely and rejected, unless it can be shown that the... 49

COMMITTEES shall lie on the table one day for consideration. All reports of.. 26

COMMITTEE of the Senate may be received to a general appropriation bill. An amendment moved by a standing or select........................ 30

COMMITTEE of the Whole, before being considered in the Senate, unless otherwise ordered. All bills on a second reading shall first be considered by the Senate as a... 28

COMMITTEE of the Whole, the Vice-President, or President pro tem., may call a member to fill the chair during the time it shall remain in Committee of the Whole, and the chairman so called shall, during such time, have the powers of a President pro tempore. When the Senate shall consider a treaty, bill, or resolution, as in...................... 28

COMMITTEE of the Whole. Should a bill on third reading be committed and reported with an amendment, it shall again be read a second time and considered in 29

COMMITTEE of the Whole. The second reading of a treaty shall be for consideration on a subsequent day in................................. 38

COMMITTEE of the Whole to be entered on the journal, but every vote of the Senate shall be entered on the journal. The proceedings of the Senate when not acting as in....................................... 33

COMMITMENT. It shall always be in order, before the final passage of any bill, &c., &c., to move its.. 29

COMMITMENT take place, and the committee report an amendment, the bill, &c., shall again be read a second time, &c. And should such....... 29

COMMUNICATIONS from the President to be kept secret, &c. Confidential. 39

CONCUR in a resolution to suspend the 16th and 17th joint rules shall always be in order, immediately considered, and decided without debate. A motion to... 53

CONFIDENTIAL business, &c., the President shall direct the gallery to be

No.

cleared. On a motion made and seconded to shut the doors on the
discussion of 18

CONFIDENTIAL or executive business, the Senate shall be cleared of all
persons except the Secretary, the principal or executive clerk, the sergeant-at-arms, and doorkeeper and the assistant doorkeeper. When
acting on... 41

CONFIDENTIAL communications made by the President of the United States
to the Senate shall be by the members thereof kept secret; and all
treaties which may be laid before the Senate shall also be kept secret
until the Senate shall, by their resolution, take off the injunction of
secrecy. All.. 39

CONFIDENCE of the Senate. Penalty of an officer or member for violating
the... 50

CONFIDENTIAL legislative proceedings of the Senate shall be kept in separate
and distinct books. The legislative proceedings, the executive proceedings, and the... 42

CONSENT. Bills may be read more than once on the same day by unanimous.. 26

CONSENT. Nominations may be considered the same day, when received
by unanimous 37

CONSIDERATION, and also reports of committees. All resolutions (not
joint) shall lie on the table one day for....................... 26

CONSIDERATION of a special order, it shall be the duty of the Chair to take
it up. When the time has arrived for the..................... 31

CONSIDERATION, they shall take precedence according to the order of time
at which they were severally assigned. When two or more subjects
shall have been specially assigned for......................... 31

CONSIDERATION. When nominations shall be made in writing by the
President of the United States to the Senate, a future day shall be
assigned, unless the Senate unanimously direct otherwise, for taking
them into 37

CONSIDERATION in Committee of the Whole and on a subsequent day. The
second reading of a treaty shall be for........................ 38

CONSIDERATION, the concurrence of two-thirds, &c., shall not be requisite,
except on the final question. When an amendment to the Constitution
is under... 44

CONSIDERED in Committee of the Whole, unless otherwise ordered. All
bills on second reading shall be............................... 28

CONSIDERED as in Committee of the Whole. Should a bill on third reading
be committed, and an amendment reported, it shall be again read a
second time and... 29

CONSIDERED, and decided without debate. A motion to suspend the 16th
and 17th joint rules shall always be in order, immediately......... 53

CONSTITUTION same as on bills, &c. Proceedings on amendments to the.. 26

CONSTITUTIONAL amendment shall be, "Whether it shall be engrossed and
read a third time." The final question on the second reading of any.. 29

No.

CONSTITUTION is under consideration, the concurrence of two-thirds of the members present shall not be requisite to decide any question for amendments, or extending to the merits, being short of the final question. When an amendment to be proposed to the.................... 44

CONTINGENT fund, if excused by the Senate. The expenses of sending for absent Senators shall be paid out of the............................. 8

CONTINGENT or any other fund shall be treated as bills, &c. All resolutions, &c., granting money out of the............................... 26

CONTINGENT fund of the Senate, or creating a charge on the same. The standing Committee to Audit and Control the Contingent Expenses of the Senate, to consist of three members, to whom shall be referred all resolutions directing the payment of money out of the............... 34

CONTINUATION of the legislative business of the Senate from session to session of a Congress...................................... 52

CONVENED by the President of the United States to any other place, the President of the Senate and Senators shall attend at the place appointed, &c. When the Senate shall be............................. 37

CONVENTIONS lawfully called of the States, not referred to the Committee on Printing. Motions to print documents from legislatures or........ 34

CONVERSATION between members not allowed to interrupt the business of the Senate.. 2

CORRECTED. The journal read at commencement of each day's session, to the end that mistakes may be.................................. 1

COURT of Claims. Whenever a private bill is under consideration, it shall be in order to move as a substitute for it a resolution of the Senate referring the case to the.. 29

D.

DEBATE shall not be interrupted by talking, reading newspapers, &c.... 2

DEBATE. No member shall interrupt another when speaking in......... 2

DEBATE shall stand in his place and address the Chair, and when finished shall sit down. Every member speaking in........................ 3

DEBATE, on same day, without leave of Senate. No member shall speak more than twice in any one... 4

DEBATE shall speak first. The member first rising in................... 5

DEBATE, subject to an appeal to the Senate. Questions of order decided by the President without... 6

DEBATE, they shall be taken down in writing, that the President may judge. When exceptionable words are spoken in................... 7

DEBATE contains several points, it may be divided, &c. If a question in.. 12

DEBATE at a third reading, unless by unanimous consent. No amendment received for discussion or... 29

DEBATE. When the yeas and nays are called, each member shall answer without.. 16

DEBATE on the merits of the question on a motion to take up a subject not allowed...

No.

DEBATE shall transgress the rules he shall be called to order. If any member in..   6

DEBATE no motion shall be received but to adjourn, &c. &c. When a question is under...   11

DEBATE. A motion for adjournment shall always be in order, and shall be determined without...   11

DEBATE. When the reading of a paper is called for and objected to, it shall be determined by a vote of the Senate and without............   14

DEBATE. A motion to suspend the 16th and 17th joint rules always in order, immediately considered, and decided without.................   53

DEBATE on business requiring secrecy, the doors shall be shut. On a....   18

DEBATED until seconded. No motion shall be............................   9

DEBATED. Motions seconded, reduced to writing if desired, delivered in at table, and read before being...................................   10

DECISION. Any motion may be withdrawn before a....................   10

DECISION is announced from the Chair, no member shall be permitted to vote. When the   17

DECISION of the President. When the Senate are equally divided, the Secretary shall take the...............................   21

DEPARTMENT may be received to a general appropriation bill. An amendment in pursuance of an estimate from the head of some executive....   30

DEPARTMENTS to be referred to the Committee on Printing. Motions to print documents from the executive...............................   34

DISTRICT of Columbia, to consist of seven members. A standing Committee on the...   34

DISCUSSION. (See *Debate.*)

DIVIDED. A question containing several points may be.................   12

DIVIDED, &c. A motion to strike out and insert shall not be...........   12

DIVIDED, the Secretary shall take the decision of the President. When the Senate are equally   21

DOCUMENT shall be printed for the Senate without special order, except a bill reported by a committee. No paper or   25

DOCUMENTS, reports, &c., the printing of which shall be moved, shall be referred to the Committee on Printing, (with exceptions as stated in rule.) (See *Rule.*) All   34

DOORS, on discussion of business requiring secrecy in the opinion of a member, the President shall order the gallery to be cleared, and the doors shall remain shut during the discussion. On a motion made and seconded to shut the...   18

DOORS of the Senate to present a petition, &c. No motion in order to admit any person within the   19

DOORS of the Senate chamber. Description of persons (and none others) who shall be admitted on the floor of or within the..................   47

DRAWINGS ordered to be printed shall be directed and procured by the Committee on Printing. Maps and.................................   34

No.

E.

ENGROSSED and read a third time." The final question on the second
reading of every bill, &c., shall be "Whether it shall be............   29
ENGROSSED Bills, to consist of three members, whose duty it shall be to
examine all bills, amendments, resolutions, or motions, before they go
out of the possession of the Senate; and shall deliver the same to the
Secretary of the Senate, who shall enter upon the journal that the same
have been correctly engrossed. A standing Committee on...........   34
ENROLLED Bills, to consist of three members. A standing Committee on.   34
EQUALLY divided, the Secretary shall take the decision of the President.
When the Senate are.....................................   21
ERRORS or mistakes may be corrected. Journal read daily, to end that
any   1
ESTIMATE from the head of a department may be received to a general
appropriation bill. An amendment in pursuance of an...............   30
ESTIMATE of the probable cost. Reports from the Committee on Printing
in favor of printing additional numbers of any document shall be ac-
companied by an..   34
EXAMINED by the committee of the Senate on. Engrossed bills of the
Senate...   34
EXCEPTIONABLE words used by a Senator; if called to order, shall be taken
down in writing   7
EXCUSE for non-attendance to be made by members sent for, or they shall
pay the expenses...   8
EXCUSED from voting. For special reason a member may be............   16
EXECUTIVE departments, to be referred to the Committee on Printing. Mo-
tions to print *documents from*   34
EXECUTIVE business to be decided without debate. Motion to proceed to
the consideration of..   11
EXECUTIVE business, the President shall direct the gallery to be cleared,
and during the discussion of such motion the doors shall remain shut.
On a motion made and seconded to shut the doors on the discussion of
any business which may, in the opinion of a member, require secrecy,
or on confidential or...   18
EXECUTIVE business. Action of the Senate on nominations and.........   37
EXECUTIVE business. Action of the Senate on treaties and...............   38
EXECUTIVE business. Secrecy enjoined on confidential and.............   39
EXECUTIVE business. Secrecy enjoined respecting information or remarks
relative to the character, &c., of persons nominated by the President,
being...   40
EXECUTIVE business, the Senate shall be cleared of all persons, except the
Secretary of the Senate, the principal or the executive clerk, the sergeant-at-arms, and doorkeeper and assistant doorkeeper. When acting
on confidential or   41

No.

EXECUTIVE clerk admitted in secret session.......................... 41

EXECUTIVE proceedings, and the confidential legislative proceedings shall be kept in separate and distinct books. The legislative proceedings, the.. 42

EXECUTIVE records of the Senate, but no further extracts from the executive journal shall be furnished except by special order. The President of the United States shall, from time to time, be furnished with an authenticated transcript of the... 43

EXPULSION of a member for violating the confidence of the Senate........ 50

EXTRACT from the executive journal shall be furnished except by special order. The President shall, from time to time, be furnished with an authenticated transcript of the executive records of the Senate, and all nominations approved or definitely acted on by the Senate shall be returned by the Secretary on the next day after such proceedings may occur, but no further... 43

F.

FILES for the purpose of referring them at a subsequent session, unless error in report or new evidence be produced. Not in order to move to take the papers of a rejected claim from the......................... 49

FILLING up blanks, the largest sum and longest time shall first be put. In 13

FINANCE, to consist of seven members. A standing Committee on....... 34

FLOOR of the Senate. Description of persons (and none others) who shall be admitted on the 47

FOREIGN Relations, to consist of seven members. A standing Committee on 34

G.

GALLERY to be cleared. On a motion made and seconded to shut the doors, the President shall order the............................... 18

GENERAL orders. Special orders to take precedence of................. 31

GRANT money out of the contingent or any other fund shall be treated as bills. All resolutions, &c., which may............................ 26

H.

HOUR has arrived for the consideration of a special order, it shall be the duty of the Chair to take it up, &c. When the..................... 31

HOUSE, the names taken alphabetically. Upon a call of the.............. 16

HOUSE of Representatives by the Secretary, who shall previously indorse the final determination of the Senate thereon. Messages shall be sent to the.. 45

I.

INDIAN Affairs, to consist of seven members. A standing Committee on.. 34

No.

INFORMATION or remarks concerning the character or qualifications of
    persons nominated, to be kept secret................................. 40
INJUNCTION of secrecy. All confidential communications and treaties
    shall be kept secret until the Senate shall, by their resolution, take off
    the.. 39
INSERT shall not be divided. A motion to strike out and............... 12
INSERT. (See *Strike Out*.) Motion to strike out and.................. 12

J.

JOINT rules always in order, be immediately considered, and be decided
    without debate. A motion to suspend the sixteenth and seventeenth.. 53
JOINT resolutions the same as on bills. Action on. (See *Bills*.)
JOURNAL of the preceding day shall be read, to the end that any mistake
    may be corrected. The President having taken the chair, and a quo-
    rum being present, the... 1
JOURNAL or papers are being read no interruption to be made. While the 2
JOURNAL is read. Morning business after the......................... 24
JOURNALS. The titles of bills and parts affected by amendments to be
    inserted on the.. 32
JOURNAL as concisely as possible, care being taken to detail a true and
    accurate account of the proceedings; but every vote of the Senate
    shall be entered on the journal, and a brief statement of the contents
    of each petition, memorial, or paper presented to the Senate, shall also
    be inserted on the journal. The proceedings of the Senate, when not
    acting as in Committee of the Whole, shall be entered on the........ 33
JOURNAL. Engrossed bills examined by the committee shall be entered by
    the Secretary of the Senate as correctly engrossed upon the.......... 34
JOURNALS. The legislative proceedings, the executive proceedings, and
    the confidential legislative proceedings of the Senate, shall be kept in
    separate and distinct books or...................................... 42
JOURNAL of the Senate; but no further extract from the executive journal
    shall be furnished except by special order. The President of the
    United States shall from time to time be furnished with an authenti-
    cated transcript of the executive records or........................ 43
JUDICIARY, to consist of seven members. A standing Committee on the.. 34

L.

LARGEST sum and longest time first put. In filling up the blanks the.... 13
LEAVE of the Senate. No member shall speak more than twice in any one
    debate, on the same day, without................................... 4
LEAVE of the Senate. A member called to order when speaking, for trans-
    gressing the rules, cannot proceed without.......................... 6
LEAVE of absence first obtained. No member shall absent himself from
    service of Senate without... 8
LEAVE of the Senate required to withdraw a motion to reconsider........ 10

No.

LEAVE to bring in a bill. One day's notice required for 25

LEGISLATIVE business to be continued from session to session of a Congress 52

LEGISLATIVE proceedings, the executive proceedings, and the confidential legislative proceedings of the Senate, shall be kept in separate and distinct books. The 42

LEGISLATURES or conventions lawfully called of the States, not referred to the Committee on Printing. Motions to print documents from the 34

LIE on the table, &c., &c., &c. When a question is under debate no motion shall be received but to 11

LIE on the table one day for consideration. All resolutions and reports of committee shall 26

LONGEST time first put. In filling up blanks the largest sum and 13

M.

MAJORITY of members present, may send for absent members. Less than a quorum, but a 8

MAJORITY may move a reconsideration. A member of the 20

MAJORITY of the whole number of votes given necessary to the appointment of a chairman of a standing committee. A 35

MAJORITY of votes. When two-thirds are requisite to carry the affirmative, any member who votes on that side which prevailed in the question may move for a reconsideration, which shall be decided by a 20

MANUFACTURES, to consist of five members. A standing Committee on.. 34

MAPS and drawings ordered to be printed shall be directed and obtained by the Committee on Printing 34

MEETINGS of the Senate. Opening or commencement of daily 1

MEETING of the Senate at the commencement or during any session, absent members may be sent for, &c. In case a less number than a quorum attend at the time to which the Senate stood adjourned, or at a 8

MEMBER shall speak to another or otherwise interrupt the business of the Senate, or read any newspaper while the journals are being read, or when any member is speaking in debate. No 2

MEMBER rising to speak shall address the Chair, stand at his place, and sit down when finished. Every 3

MEMBER shall speak more than twice in any one debate, on the same day, without leave of the Senate. No 4

MEMBERS rise to speak the President shall name the one to speak first; but in all cases the member rising and addressing the Chair first shall speak first. When two 5

MEMBER may call another to order who shall transgress the rules. Any.. 6

MEMBER called to order for transgressing the rules shall sit down and not proceed without leave. Any 6

MEMBER called to order by a Senator shall be taken down in writing, to enable the President to judge. The exceptionable words of a 7

MEMBER shall absent himself from the service of the Senate without leave of the Senate first obtained, &c. No 8

No.

MEMBERS present, may send for absent members. Less than a quorum, but a majority of the   8

MEMBERS. The sergeant-at-arms, or other authorized person, may be sent for absent...   8

MEMBER. A motion seconded shall be reduced to writing, if desired by a.   10

MEMBER may have a question containing several points divided. A   12

MEMBER, it shall be determined by a vote of the Senate without debate. When the reading of a paper is called for, and objected to by a.......   14

MEMBERS present may call for the yeas and nays. One-fifth of the   16

MEMBERS to be taken alphabetically. In taking yeas and nays, or on a call of the House, the names of the...................................   16

MEMBER shall answer without debate unless, for special reason, he be excused. When the yeas and nays are called, each....................   16

MEMBER permitted to vote after decision is announced from the Chair. When a question is taken by yeas and nays no......................   17

MEMBER, require secrecy, the doors shall, on his motion, when seconded, be shut. On the discussion of business which may, in the opinion of a.   18

MEMBER of the majority may move a reconsideration. A   20

MEMBERS shall signify their assent or dissent by answering aye or no. The President of the Senate shall put every question, either in presence or absence of the President of the United States, and the   22

MEMBER to the chair, not to extend beyond an adjournment. The appointment by the President of a...   23

MEMBER, before presenting a petition, &c., to make a brief verbal statement of its contents. A..   24

MEMBER shall object at the time to the reference of a petition, as matter of course, then the question on reference to be taken. When a.........   24

MEMBER to fill the chair while the Senate is in Committee of the Whole. The Vice-President or President pro tempore may call a..............   28

MEMBERS present. On the third reading of any bill, &c., no amendment shall be received unless by the unanimous consent of the   29

MEMBERS shall attend at the place appointed. When the Senate shall be convened by the President of the United States to any other place, the President of the Senate and.......................................   37

MEMBER shall be free to move an amendment to a treaty on its second reading, &c. Every...   38

MEMBERS present shall be requisite to decide a question affirmatively. In proceedings upon treaties two-thirds of the   38

MEMBER shall again be free to move amendments, &c. When the proceedings on a treaty shall be reduced to the form of a ratification, every...   38

MEMBERS thereof, be kept secret until the Senate shall, by their resolution, take off the injunction of secrecy. All confidential communications and treaties laid before the Senate by the President shall, by the   39

MEMBERS present shall not be requisite to decide any question for amendments, or extending to the merits, being short of the final question. When an amendment to be proposed to the Constitution is under consideration, the concurrence of two-thirds of the......................   44

No.

MEMBER who votes on that side which prevailed may move for a reconsideration, which shall be decided by a majority of votes. When two-thirds are requisite, any 20

MEMBERS of the Senate shall be allowed on the floor of the Senate during a session, except those specified in this rule. No persons but 47

MEMBER of the Senate convicted of disclosing for publication any written or printed matter directed by the Senate to be held in confidence, shall be liable, if an officer, to dismissal from the service of the Senate, and in the case of a member, to suffer expulsion from the body. Any officer or 50

MEMORIAL, or address, or hear any such read. No motion shall be in order to admit any person within the doors of the Senate chamber to read a petition 19

MEMORIAL or petition shall be presented, and before being received and read at the table, a brief statement of its contents shall be verbally made. At the time when a 24

MEMORIAL, or paper, shall be inserted on the journal. A brief statement of the contents of each petition 33

MEMORIAL stating how the committee have erred, or that new evidence has been discovered, &c. Not in order to take papers of a rejected claim from the files for reference, unless the claimant shall present a 49

MEMORIALS, &c. (See Petitions.)

MESSAGES shall be sent to the House of Representatives by the Secretary, who shall previously indorse the final determination of the Senate thereon 45

MESSENGERS are introduced at any stage of business, except while a question is being put, while the yeas and nays are being called, or while the ballots are being counted 46

MILITARY Affairs and the Militia, to consist of seven members. A standing Committee on 34

MINES and Mining, to consist of seven members. A standing Committee on 34

MINUTES of the Senate. When the Senate shall be convened by the President in any other place, the Secretary of the Senate shall also attend to take the 37

MISTAKE may be corrected. Journal to be read, to the end that any 1

MONEY out of the contingent or any other fund shall be treated as bills. All resolutions, &c., which may grant 26

MORNING business. Business at the commencement of the session, or 1

MORNING business after the journal is read. Order of the 24

MOTION shall be debated until seconded. No 9

MOTION made and seconded shall be written, if desired, delivered in at the table, and read before debated. A 10

MOTION may be withdrawn before decision, amendment, or ordering of yeas and nays, except a motion to reconsider, which shall not be withdrawn without leave. A 10

No.

MOTION shall be received but to—1, adjourn ; 2, to lie on the table; 3, to
    postpone indefinitely ; 4, to postpone to a day certain ; 5, to commit ;
    or, 6, to amend, in the order here stated.   When a question is under
    debate no 11
MOTION for adjournment shall always be in order, and shall be decided
    without debate. A 11
MOTION to strike out and insert shall not be divided. A 12
MOTION to strike out and insert one proposition shall not prevent a motion
    to strike out and insert a different proposition, nor a motion simply to
    strike out ; nor shall the rejection of a motion to strike out prevent a
    motion to strike out and insert. A 12
MOTION in filling blanks is for largest sum and longest time.   The privi-
    leged 13
MOTION made and seconded to shut the doors, &c., the President shall
    direct the gallery to be cleared.   On a 18
MOTION not in order to admit any person in Senate to present any petition,
    memorial, or address, or to hear any such read. A 19
MOTION for reconsideration may be made by one of a majority before sub-
    ject has gone out of possession of Senate, if made same day or within
    two next days of actual session thereafter. A 20
MOTION for reconsideration not in order after subject has gone out of pos-
    session of the Senate, except a resolution confirming or rejecting a
    nomination, nor after two days of actual session from time of vote. A. 20
MOTION to reconsider a nomination, where the resolution confirming or re-
    jecting it has been sent to the President, shall always be accompanied
    by a motion requesting the President to return the same to the Senate. A 20
MOTION for leave to bring in a bill.   One day's notice at least shall be given
    of a 25
MOTION to suspend, or to concur in a resolution of the House of Repre-
    sentatives to suspend, the 16th and 17th joint rules, or either of them,
    shall always be in order, be immediately considered, and be decided
    without debate. A 53
MOTION requiring three readings previous to being passed shall be
    "Whether it shall be engrossed and read a third time?"   The final
    question on any 29
MOTIONS to print certain documents, referred to the Committee on Printing 34
MOTIONS to print other documents and bills, not referred to the Committee
    on Printing 34
MOTIONS to print additional documents, referred to the Committee on
    Printing 34
MOTIONS to print by order of standing committees, not referred to the
    Committee on Printing 34
MOTION, be referred to such committee.   When any subject or matter
    shall have been referred to a committee, any other subject or matter of
    a similar nature may, on 35

No.

MOTIONS are made for reference of the same subject to a select committee, and to a standing committee, the question on reference to the standing committee shall first be put. When 36

MOTION to reject, ratify, or modify a treaty on the first reading shall be received. No 38

MOTION for reconsideration, and it shall be decided by a majority of votes. When a question is decided by two-thirds, any member on the side that prevailed may make a... 20

N.

NAYS. (See *Yeas and Nays.*)

NAVAL Affairs, to consist of seven members. A standing Committee on... 34

NEWSPAPER, &c., while the journal is being read, or a member is speaking. No member shall read any... 2

NOMINATIONS confirmed or rejected may be reconsidered after the resolution announcing the decision of the Senate has been sent to the President; but all motions to reconsider such nominations must be accompanied by a motion requesting the President to return the same to the Senate. 20

NOMINATIONS shall be made in writing by the President of the United States to the Senate, a future day shall be assigned, unless the Senate unanimously direct otherwise, for taking them into consideration. When.. 37

NOMINATIONS neither approved nor rejected during the session at which they are made, shall not be acted upon at any succeeding session without being again made by the President.............................. 37

NOMINATED by the President to office shall be kept secret. All information or remarks touching or concerning the character or qualifications of any person.. 40

NOMINATIONS approved or definitely acted on by the Senate shall be returned to the President by the Secretary on the next day after such proceedings may occur, unless otherwise ordered.................... 43

NOTICE, at least, shall be given of an intended motion for leave to bring in a bill, &c. One day's... 25

NOTICE at each reading of a bill or joint resolution, &c. The President shall give... 26

O.

OATH or affirmation prescribed by act of July 2, 1862, to be taken and subscribed by every Senator, and by the Secretary, in open Senate, before entering upon their duties................................... 51

OBJECTED to by a member at the time, the question on reference to be taken. When the reference of a petition, &c., as a matter of course, is.. 24

OBJECTION is made to reading a paper, it shall be determined by a vote of the Senate, and without debate. When 14

OFFICER or member of the Senate convicted of disclosing for publication any written or printed matter directed by the Senate to be held in con-

No.

fidence, shall be liable, if an officer, to dismissal from the service of
the Senate, and, in the case of a member, to suffer expulsion from the
body. Any..   50
ORDER shall not be interrupted by talking or reading newspapers, &c....   2
ORDER shall be decided by the President, without debate, subject to an
appeal to the Senate. Every question of   6
ORDER. The Chair may call for the sense of the Senate on any question of   6
ORDER for transgressing the rules. The Chair shall, or a member may,
call another to..   6
ORDER shall sit down and not proceed without leave of the Senate. A
member called to...   6
ORDER by a Senator shall be taken down in writing to enable the President
to judge. The exceptionable words of a member called to...........   7
ORDER, and decided without debate. A motion for adjournment shall
always be in...   11
ORDER to move for a division of the question. On motion to strike out
and insert, it shall not be in.....................................   12
ORDER to admit any person in Senate to present a petition, &c. No motion in..   19
ORDER for a member of the majority to move a reconsideration, &c., within
two days of actual session, if the matter is still in possession of the
Senate. It is in..   20
ORDER to move the reconsideration of a subject which has gone out of pos-
session of the Senate, or when two next days of actual session shall
have elapsed. It is not in   20
ORDER to move the commitment of a bill, &c., before its final passage.
It shall always be in   29
ORDER to move, as a substitute for it, a resolution of the Senate referring
the case to the Court of Claims. Whenever a private bill is under
consideration, it shall be in......................................   29
ORDER, &c. A motion to suspend the 16th and 17th joint rules always in   53
ORDER to move to take the papers of rejected claims from the files for the
purpose of reference, without error in report or new evidence being
produced. Not in   49
ORDERS of the day. The unfinished business at preceding adjournment
shall have preference in the special...............................   15
ORDER of special orders assigned, regulated, and fixed, and given precedence over general orders. The....................................   31
ORDER, special, not to be made without the concurrence of two-thirds
present   31
ORDER of the Senate for that purpose. No paper, except original treaties,
&c., shall be returned or delivered from the office of the Secretary
without an...   43
ORDER. An authenticated transcript of the executive records of the Senate
shall be furnished, from time to time, to the President of the United
States, but no further extract of the executive journal shall be furnished
except by special   43

No.

ORDERED. All bills on second reading shall be considered in Committee of the Whole before being considered in the Senate, unless otherwise.. 28

P.

PACIFIC Railroad, to consist of nine members. A standing Committee on 34

PAPERS are being read no interruption to be made. While public......... 2

PAPER is called for and objected to, it will be decided by a vote of the Senate, and without debate. When the reading of a.................. 14

PAPER or document shall be printed for the use of the Senate without special order, &c. No 25

PAPER, except original treaties, &c., shall be returned or delivered from the office of the Secretary without an order of the Senate for that purpose. No 43

PAPERS of a rejected claim from the files for the purpose of referring them at a subsequent session, unless error in report or new evidence be produced. Not in order to move to take........................... 49

PASSAGE of a bill, &c., to move its commitment, &c. It shall always be in order before the final... 29

PASSAGES as are or may be set apart for the use of the Senate and its officers. The Presiding Officer of the Senate shall have the regulation of such parts of the Capitol and of its 48

PASSED, &c. Every bill and joint resolution shall receive three readings previous to being 26

PATENTS and the Patent Office, to consist of five members. A standing Committee on 34

PENALTY of an officer or member for violating the confidence of the Senate 50

PENSIONS, to consist of seven members. A standing Committee on....... 34

PERSON or persons within doors of Senate to present any petition, memorial, or address, or to hear any such read. No motion in order to admit any 19

PERSON nominated to office by the President shall be kept secret. All information or remarks touching or concerning the character or qualification of any.. 40

PERSONS, except as stated in the rule. When acting on confidential or executive business, the Senate shall be cleared of all................. 41

PERSONS (and none others) who shall be admitted on the floor of the Senate. Description of 47

PETITION, memorial, or address, or hear any such read. No motion in order to admit any person in the Senate chamber to present a........ 19

PETITIONS, memorials, or papers, first called for in morning business, a brief statement of their contents to be made before reception, &c., and referred, of course, unless objected to, and then question taken....... 24

PETITION, memorial, or paper presented to the Senate shall be inserted on the journal. A brief statement of the contents of each............... 33

PLURALITY of votes sufficient for the appointment of all other committees than the chairman of standing committees, for whose appointment a majority is necessary... 35

No.

POINTS may be divided. A question containing several.................. 12

POSITION on the calendar according to the order of time *for* which and *at* which they were assigned, and not to lose their position on account of intervening adjournments, &c. Special orders to have.............. 31

POST Offices and Post Roads, to consist of seven members. A standing Committee on 34

POSTPONE indefinitely, to a day certain, &c. &c. (See *Rule.*) When a question is under debate, no motion shall be received but to.......... 11

POSTPONE to a day certain, &c. (See *Rule.*) When a question is under debate, no motion shall be received but to......................... 11

POSTPONED by direction of the Senate. Special orders to have precedence over general orders, unless...: 31

POWERS of a President *pro tempore,* &c. The chairman of a Committee of the Whole to have the.. 28

PRECEDENCE of motions admissible, when a question is under debate, viz: 1, to adjourn; 2, to lie on the table; 3, to postpone indefinitely; 4, to postpone to a day certain; 5, to commit; or, 6, to amend............. 11

PRECEDENCE of special orders according to the order of time *for* which they were assigned, and *at* which they were assigned, and over general orders, &c. (See *Rule*)... 31

PREFERENCE in the special orders, &c. The unfinished business shall have the 15

PRESIDENT of the Senate having taken the chair, and a quorum being present, the business proceeds. The.................................... 1

PRESIDENT shall be addressed by every member rising to speak. The.... 3

PRESIDENT shall name the person to speak; but in all cases the member rising and addressing the Chair first shall speak first. When two members rise at the same time the..................................... 5

PRESIDENT shall call any member to order for transgression of rules. The 6

PRESIDENT without debate, subject to appeal to Senate. Questions of order shall be decided by the... 6

PRESIDENT may call for the sense of the Senate on any question of order. The...: 6

PRESIDENT to judge when a member is called to order for exceptionable words, by their being taken down, in writing. The..................... 7

PRESIDENT. A motion made and seconded shall be reduced to writing if desired by the.. 10

PRESIDENT, or the Chair, no member shall be permitted to vote. When a decision is announced by the... 17

PRESIDENT shall direct the gallery to be cleared, &c. On a motion made and seconded to shut the doors the................................... 18

PRESIDENT. When the Senate are equally divided the Secretary shall take the decision of the.. 21

PRESIDENT of the Senate shall put all questions in the presence or absence of the President of the United States. The........................... 22

No.

PRESIDENT of the Senate *pro tempore*, shall have the right to name a member to perform the duties of the chair, but such substitution shall not extend beyond an adjournment. The Vice-President of the United States, or the... 23

PRESIDENT shall make a brief verbal statement of the contents of petitions, &c., presented by him. The... 24

PRESIDENT shall first call for petitions, &c. (See *Rule*.) In the morning business the.. 24

PRESIDENT shall give notice at each reading of a bill or joint resolution whether it be the first, second, or third. The........................ 26

PRESIDENT *pro tempore*, may call a member to fill the chair, &c. When the Senate shall consider a treaty, bill, or resolution as in Committee of the Whole, the Vice-President, or... 28

PRESIDENT of the Senate, or the Chair, to take up such special order, and it shall be considered unless postponed by a vote of the Senate. When the hour has arrived for the consideration of a special order, it shall be the duty of the.. 31

PRESIDENT of the Senate shall have a chair on the floor, be considerd as the head of the Senate, and his chair shall be assigned to the President of the United States. When the President of the United States shall meet the Senate in the Senate chamber, the.......................... 37

PRESIDENT of the Senate and Senators shall attend at the place appointed, &c. (See *Rule*.) When the Senate shall be convened by the President of the United States to any other place, the........................... 37

PRESIDING Officer of the Senate shall have the regulation of such parts of the Capitol, and of its passages, as are or may be set apart for the use of the Senate and its officers. The.................................... 48

PRESIDENT of the United States. The President of the Senate shall put all questions in the presence or absence of the.......................... 22

PRESIDENT of the United States may be requisite, shall be treated as bills. All resolutions, &c., to which the approbation and signature of the ... 26

PRESIDENT of the United States to the Senate, a future day shall be assigned, unless the Senate unanimously direct otherwise, for taking them into consideration. When nominations shall be made in writing by the... 37

PRESIDENT of the United States. Nominations neither approved nor rejected during the session at which they are made, shall not be acted upon at any succeeding session without being again made by the 37

PRESIDENT of the United States shall meet the Senate in the Senate chamber, the President of the Senate shall have a chair on the floor, be considered the head of the Senate, and his chair shall be assigned to the President of the United States. When the 37

PRESIDENT of the United States to any other place, the President of the Senate and Senators shall attend at the place appointed. The Secretary of the Senate shall also attend to take the minutes of the Senate. When the Senate shall be convened by the................................ 37

5

No.

PRESIDENT of the United States shall be kept secret. All confidential communications and treaties from the................................... 39

PRESIDENT of the United States. Doors to be closed and secret session held on motion by a member when desired by the (joint rule)........ 22

PRESIDENT to office shall be kept secret. All information or remarks touching or concerning the character or qualifications of any person , nominated by the... 40

PRESIDENT of the United States shall, from time to time, be furnished with an authenticated transcript of the executive records of the Senate; and all *nominations* approved or definitely acted on by the Senate shall be returned by the Secretary on the next day after such action is had unless otherwise ordered by the Senate; but *no further extract* from the executive journal shall be furnished, except by special order; and *no paper*, except original treaties, transmitted by the President of the United States or any executive officer, *shall be returned* or delivered from the office of the Secretary without an order from the Senate for that purpose. The.. 43

PRINTED for the use of the Senate. All bills reported by a committee shall, after the first reading, be 25

PRINTED for the use of the Senate without special order. But no other paper or document (than as above) shall be......................... 25

PRINTING, to consist of three members, to whom shall be referred every question on the printing of documents, reports, or other matter transmitted by either of the executive departments, and all memorials, petitions, accompanying documents, together with all other matter, the printing of which shall be moved, *excepting bills originating in Congress, resolutions offered by any Senator, communications from the legislatures or conventions lawfully called of the respective States, and motions to print by order of the standing committees of the Senate;* motions to print additional numbers shall likewise be referred to said committee; and when the report shall be in favor of printing additional numbers, it shall be accompanied by an estimate of the probable cost; the said committee shall also supervise and direct the procuring of maps and drawings accompanying documents ordered to be printed. A Committee on 34

PRINTING shall also supervise and direct the procuring of maps and drawings accompanying documents ordered to be printed. The standing Committee on 34

PRIVATE bill is under consideration it shall be in order to move, as a substitute for it, a resolution of the Senate referring the case to the Court of Claims. Whenever a... 29

PRIVATE claim, unless it be to carry out the provisions of some existing law or treaty stipulation. No amendment shall be received to any general appropriation bill whose object is to provide for a 30

PRIVATE Land Claims, to consist of five members. A standing Committee on 34

No.

PRIVILEGED motions, when a question is under debate, and the order of their precedence... 11
PRIVILEGE of admission on the floor of the Senate. Description of persons allowed the...... 47
PROCEEDINGS on them, in the Senate, as bills, &c. All joint resolutions, and resolutions granting money, shall be treated in the.............:.... 26
PROCEEDINGS of Senate, when not acting as in Committee of the Whole, to be entered on the journal, but every vote of the Senate shall be entered on the journal, &c. (See *Rule*)............................ 33
PROCEEDINGS of the Senate shall be kept in separate and distinct books. The legislative proceedings, the executive proceedings, and the confidential legislative...................................... 42
PUBLIC Buildings and Grounds, to consist of five members, who shall have power to act jointly with the same committee of the House of Representatives. A standing Committee on the 34
PUBLIC Lands, to consist of seven members. A standing Committee on the. 34

Q.

QUALIFICATIONS of persons nominated to be kept secret. Any remarks concerning the... 40
QUESTIONS of order decided by the President without debate, subject to appeal, and the Chair may call for the sense of the Senate upon them. 6
QUESTION is under debate no motion shall be received, except to adjourn, &c., &c. (See *Rule*.) When a................................... 11
QUESTION in debate contains several points, any member may have the same divided When a.. 12
QUESTION. On motion to strike out and insert, it shall not be in order to move for a division of the... 12
QUESTION taken by yeas and nays each member shall vote, unless for special reasons he be excused. On every.......................... 16
QUESTION. When yeas and nays are called, each member shall declare openly, and without debate, his assent or dissent to the.............. 16
QUESTION, no member shall be permitted to vote, &c. (See *Rule*.) When the decision shall have been announced from the Chair on a......... 17
QUESTION decided may be reconsidered, on motion by one of the majority, if made before the subject has gone out of possession of the Senate, and if made on same day or within two next days of actual session. A.... 20
QUESTIONS shall be put by the President of the Senate, in the presence or absence of the President of the United States, and the Senators shall answer aye or no. All 22
QUESTION, unless objected to, and then question on reference taken. Reference of petitions, &c., to be made as a matter of course without 24
QUESTION upon the second reading of every bill, resolution, &c., requiring three readings, shall be, "Whether it shall be engrossed and read a third time?" The final 29

No.

QUESTION shall be again put, "Whether it shall be engrossed and read a
third time?" Should a bill on third reading be committed and an
amendment reported, it shall again be read a second time, and the   29

QUESTION on the printing of documents, reports, or other matter, (except
as stated in the rule,) shall be referred to the Committee on Printing.
Every   34

QUESTION on reference to the standing committee shall first be put. When
motions are made for reference of the same subject to a select committee
and to a standing committee, the   36

QUESTIONS on amendments to, and ratifications of treaties, (see *Rule*.)
Forms of   33

QUESTION for amendments, or extending to the merits, being short of the
final question. When an amendment of the Constitution is under
consideration the concurrence of two-thirds shall not be requisite to
decide any   44

QUESTION may have been decided by the Senate, in which two-thirds of
the members present are necessary to carry the affirmative, any member
who votes on that side which prevailed in the question may be at liberty
to move for a reconsideration; and a motion for reconsideration shall
be decided by a majority of votes. When any   20

QUESTION may move for a reconsideration, which shall be decided by a
majority of votes. When two-thirds are requisite, any member who
votes on that side which prevailed in the   20

QUESTION is being put, while the yeas and nays are being called, or while
the ballots are being counted. Messengers are introduced in any state
of business, except while a   46

QUORUM being present, the business will proceed. The President having
taken the chair, and a   1

QUORUM, but a majority of those present, may send for absent Senators,
who shall pay the expenses, unless excused when a quorum is convened. A less number than a   8

R.

RATIFICATION of treaty, (see *Treaty*—see *Rule*)   33

RATIFICATION of amendments to treaties and of treaties. Questions on.
(See *Rule*)   38

READ, to the end that any mistakes may be corrected. The chair being
taken, and a quorum present, the journal will be   1

READ any newspaper, while journals or public papers are being read, or a
member is speaking, &c. No member shall speak to another, or otherwise interrupt the business of the Senate, or   2

READ, no interruption to be made. While the journal or public papers
are being   2

READ before debated. A motion seconded shall be written if desired, delivered in at table, and   10

No.

READ. No person shall be admitted in the Senate to present any petition, address, &c., or hear any such ... 19

READ at the table. A brief statement of petitions, memorials, or papers to be made before being received or ... 24

READ. [Morning] business after the journal is ... 24

READ, after which it may be referred to a committee. No bill shall be committed until it shall have been twice ... 27

READ a third time?" The final question on the second reading of every bill, &c., shall be, "Whether it shall be engrossed and ... 29

READ a second time, &c. Should a bill, &c., on third reading, be committed and an amendment reported, it shall again be ... 29

READ a first time for information only. Every treaty ... 38

READING of a paper is called for and objected to, it shall be determined by a vote of the Senate and without debate. When the ... 14

READING. All bills reported by a committee to be printed after the first.. 25

READINGS previous to its being passed, and the President shall give notice whether it be the first, second, or third; which readings shall be on different days, unless the Senate unanimously direct otherwise. Every bill shall receive three ... 26

READING shall first be considered in Committee of the Whole before being taken up in Senate, unless otherwise ordered. All bills on second.... 28

READING of any bill, resolution, &c., requiring three readings, shall be, "Whether it shall be engrossed and read a third time?" The final question upon the second ... 29

READING of any bill, &c., unless by unanimous consent; but it may be committed, &c. No amendment received at a third ... 29

READING of a treaty shall be on a subsequent day, for consideration in Committee of the Whole. The second ... 38

RECEIVED or read at the table. A brief statement of petitions, memorials, or papers to be made before being ... 24

RECEIVED at the third reading of any bill, &c., unless by unanimous consent. No amendment ... 29

RECONSIDER shall not be withdrawn without leave. A motion to ... 10

RECONSIDERATION not in order after a bill, resolution, message, report, amendment, or motion, upon which the vote was taken, shall have gone out of the possession of the Senate, announcing the decision, except a resolution confirming or rejecting a nomination. A motion for.. 20

RECONSIDERATION shall not be in order unless made on same day the vote was taken, or within the two next days of actual session of the Senate thereafter. A motion for ... 20

RECONSIDERATION of a nomination, if the resolution announcing the decision of the Senate has been sent to the President, shall always be accompanied by a motion requesting the President to return the same to the Senate. A motion for ... 20

RECONSIDERATION of a question decided may be made, on motion by one of the majority, before the subject has gone out of the possession of the

No.

Senate, if made same day or within two next days of actual session thereafter. A.. 20

RECONSIDERATION; and a motion for reconsideration shall be decided by a majority of votes. When any question may have been decided by the Senate, in which two-thirds of the members present are necessary to carry the affirmative, any member who votes on that side which prevailed in the question may be at liberty to move for a............. 20

RECORD of the Senate; but no further extract from the executive journal shall be furnished, except by special order, &c. The President of the United States shall, from time to time, be furnished with an authenticated transcript of the executive..................................... 43

REFERENCE of petitions, memorials, and papers to committees, made as a matter of course, unless objected to, and then the question to be taken on the reference.............. 24

REFERENCE to the standing committee shall first be put. When motions are made for reference of the same subject to a select committee and to a standing committee, the question on............................... 36

REFERRED to a committee. No bill shall be committed or amended until twice read, after which it may be................................... 27

REFERRED to the Committee to Audit and Control the Contingent Expenses of the Senate. Resolutions for payment of money out of, or creating a charge on, the contingent fund of the Senate shall be................. 34

REFERRED to a committee, any other subject or matter of a similar nature may, on motion, be referred to such committee. When any subject or matter shall have been... 35

REFERRING them at subsequent sessions, unless error be stated to exist in the report, or new evidence be produced. Not in order to move to take papers or rejected claims from the files for the purpose of............. 49

REGULATION of such parts of the Capitol as may be set apart for the use of the Senate and its officers. The Presiding Officer of the Senate shall have the.. 48

REJECTED claim from the files for reference, unless error in report or new evidence be produced. Not in order to take the papers of a........... 49

REMARKS touching or concerning the character or qualifications of any person nominated by the President to office shall be kept secret. All information or.. 40

REPORTED by the committee, the bill, &c., shall again be read a second time, &c. Should a bill on the third reading be committed, and an amendment be.. 29

REPORTS of committees to be called for after petitions in morning business. 24

REPORTS of committees shall lie on the table one day for consideration. All 26

REPORTS of the Committee on Printing, in favor of printing additional numbers, to be accompanied by an estimate of the cost.............. 34

REPORT of a committee, in writing, adverse to a claim to preclude its renewal, without error be shown in report, or new evidence produced, &c...

No.

RESOLUTION, as in Committee of the Whole, a chairman may be appointed, &c. When the Senate shall consider a............................ 28

RESOLUTION, &c., requiring three readings, shall be, "Whether it shall be engrossed and read a third time?" The final question on the second reading of any bill... 29

RESOLUTIONS on third reading to be amended only by unanimous consent. 29

RESOLUTION of ratification of treaties. Forms of questions and proceedings on (see *Rule*).. 38

RESOLUTION take off the injunction of secrecy. The Senate may by..... 39

RESOLUTIONS proposing amendments to the Constitution, or to which the approbation of the President may be necessary, or which may grant money out of the contingent or any other fund, shall be treated, in all respects, in the introduction and form of proceedings on them in the Senate, in a similar manner with bills. All............................ 26

RESOLUTIONS (than the above) shall lie on the table one day for consideration, and also reports of committees. All other.................... 26

RESOLUTIONS directing the payment of money out of the contingent fund of the Senate, or creating a charge on the same, shall be referred to the Committee to Audit and Control the Contingent Expenses....... 34

RESOLUTIONS the same as on bills. Action on joint. (See *Bills.*)

REVOLUTIONARY Claims, to consist of five members. A standing Committee on.. 34

RULES, the President shall, or a member may, call to order. When a member shall transgress the............................... 6

RULES. One day's notice required for a motion to amend, suspend, or modify a rule... 53

S.

SEAT, or sit down. When a member has finished speaking he shall take his.. 3

SECONDED. No motion shall be debated until the same shall be......... 9

SECONDED shall be written, if desired by the President. Motions........ 10

SECONDED to shut the doors, the gallery shall be cleared, &c. On a motion made and... 18

SECRECY, the President shall order the gallery to be cleared, and the doors shall remain shut during the discussion. On motion made and seconded to shut the doors, on discussion of business which may, in the opinion of a member, require....................................... 18

SECRECY of the Senate. Penalty of an officer or member for violating the injunction of... 50

SECRET; and all treaties which may be laid before the Senate shall also be kept secret until the Senate shall, by their resolution, take off the injunction of secrecy. All confidential communications made by the President of the United States to the Senate shall be, by the members thereof, kept... 39

No.

SECRET. All information or remarks touching or concerning the character or qualifications of any person nominated by the President to office shall be kept a.. 40

SECRETARY shall take the decision of the President. When the Senate are equally divided, the.. 21

SECRETARY of the Senate shall enter engrossed bills as correctly engrossed upon the journal. The.. 34

SECRETARY of the Senate shall also attend to take the minutes of the Senate. When the Senate shall be convened by the President of the United States to any other place, the President of the Senate and Senators shall attend at the place appointed ; the.................... 37

SECRETARY, the principal or executive clerk, the sergeant-at-arms, and doorkeeper, and the assistant doorkeeper. When acting on confidential or executive business, the Senate shall be cleared of all persons, except the... 41

SECRETARY, on the next day after such proceedings may occur, shall return to the President of the United States all nominations approved or definitely acted on by the Senate..................................... 43

SECRETARY without an order of the Senate for that purpose. No paper, except original treaties, transmitted to the Senate by the President of the United States or any executive officer, shall be returned or delivered from the office of the...................................... 43

SECRETARY, who shall previously indorse the final determination of the Senate thereon. Messages shall be sent to the House of Representatives by the... 45

SECRETARY and other officers of the Senate to take and subscribe the oath prescribed by the act of July 2, 1862................................. 51

SELECT committee and to a standing committee, the question on reference to the standing committee shall first be put. When motions are made for reference of the same subject to a............................... 36

SENATE each day. Preliminary proceedings on the assembling of the.... 1

SENATE. No member shall speak to another, or otherwise interrupt the business of the.. 2

SENATE. No member shall speak more than twice in any one debate, on same day, without leave of the.................................... 4

SENATE. Any member called to order shall sit down, and not proceed without leave of the.. 6

SENATE. Every question of order decided by the President, without debate, subject to an appeal to the....................................... 6

SENATE he shall be called to order, &c. If any member transgress the rules of the... 6

SENATE on any question of order. The President may call for the sense of the... 6

SENATE may send for absent members. A less number than a quorum of the.. 8

No.

SENATE shall convene they may send for absent members. In case a less number than a quorum of the. (See *Rule*)............................   8

SENATE without leave first obtained. No member shall absent himself from the service of the...   8

SENATE when a quorum is convened. Excuse by absent members to be made to the...   8

SENATE. A motion to reconsider shall not be withdrawn without leave of the..   10

SENATE and without debate. When the reading of a paper is called for and objected to it shall be determined by a vote of the................   14

SENATE was engaged at the last preceding adjournment shall have preference in the special orders of the day. The unfinished business in which the...   15

SENATE may for special reason excuse a member from voting. The......   16

SENATE or House the names taken alphabetically. Upon a call of the....   16

SENATE on business requiring secrecy, the gallery shall be cleared, &c. On a motion made and seconded to shut the doors of the.............   18

SENATE chamber to present any petition, memorial, or address, or to hear any such read. No motion in order to admit any person whatsoever within the doors of the..   19

SENATE. A motion to reconsider not in order when the matter has gone out of the possession of the..   20

SENATE are equally divided, the Secretary shall take the decision of the President. When the...   21

SENATE shall be received and read at the table, a brief verbal statement of its contents shall be made by the President or the member introducing it. Before any petition, &c., addressed to the. (See *Rule*)..........   24

SENATE. All bills reported by a committee after first reading shall be printed for the use of the...   25

SENATE without special order. No paper or document, except a bill reported by a committee, shall be printed for the use of the.............   25

SENATE in a similar manner with bills. All joint resolutions, and those granting money, shall be treated in proceedings on them in..........   26

SENATE unanimously direct otherwise. Every bill shall receive three readings, on different days, unless the..................................   26

SENATE shall consider a treaty, bill, or resolution, as in Committee of the Whole, the Vice-President or President *pro tempore* may call a member to fill the chair, &c. When the   28

SENATE in the same manner as if the Senate were in Committee of the Whole, before they shall be taken up and proceeded on by the Senate, agreeably to the standing rules, unless otherwise ordered. All bills, on a second reading, shall be considered by the.....................   28

SENATE during that session, or moved by direction of a committee of the Senate, &c., may be received to a general appropriation bill. An amendment to carry out the provisions of any act or resolution passed by the...   30

No.

SENATE shall proceed to consider a special order taken up, unless postponed by vote of the Senate. The... 31

SENATE. Special orders shall not lose their position on the calendar, except by direction of the.. 31

SENATE. Special orders to have precedence over general orders, unless postponed by a vote of the.. 31

SENATE, when not acting as in Committee of the Whole, shall be entered on the journal as concisely as possible, care being taken to detail a true and accurate account of the proceedings; but every vote of the Senate shall be entered on the journal, and a brief statement of the contents of each petition, memorial, or paper presented to the Senate shall also be inserted on the journal. The proceedings of the.................. 33

SENATE. The Committee on Engrossed Bills shall examine all bills, amendments, resolutions, or motions, before they go out of the possession of the.. 34

SENATE will proceed by ballot to appoint the chairmen of standing committees, and the other members, and also all other committees. The. (See *Rule*)... 35

SENATE, a future day shall be assigned, unless the Senate unanimously direct otherwise, for taking them into consideration. When nominations shall be made in writing by the President of the United States to the.. 37

SENATE in the Senate chamber, the President of the Senate shall have a chair on the floor, be considered as the head of the Senate, and his chair shall be assigned to the President of the United States. When the President of the United States shall meet the...................... 37

SENATE shall be convened by the President of the United States to any other place, the President of the Senate and Senators shall attend at the place appointed. The Secretary of the Senate shall also attend to take the minutes of the Senate. When the.......................... 37

SENATE on treaties communicated by the President. Proceedings of the 38

SENATE shall be by the members thereof kept secret until the Senate remove the injunction of secrecy. All treaties and confidential communications made by the President of the United States to the........... 39

SENATE relative to the character or qualifications of any person nominated to office shall be kept secret. All information or remarks made in the 40

SENATE shall be cleared of all persons, except the Secretary and the principal or the executive clerk, the sergeant-at-arms, and doorkeeper and assistant doorkeeper. When acting on confidential or executive business, the... 41

SENATE shall be kept in separate and distinct books. The legislative proceedings, the executive proceedings, and the confidential legislative proceedings of the... 42

SENATE shall be returned by the Secretary on the next day after such action is had, &c. All nominations approved or definitely acted on by the... 43

No.

SENATE for that purpose. No paper, except original treaties, transmitted to the Senate by the President of the United States, or any executive officer, shall be returned or delivered from the office of the Secretary without an order of the... 43

SENATE, &c. The President of the United States shall, from time to time, be furnished with an authenticated transcript of the executive records of the... 43

SENATE thereon. Messages shall be sent to the House of Representatives by the Secretary, who shall previously indorse the final determination of the... 45

SENATE. Description of persons (and none others) who shall be admitted on the floor of the... 47

SENATE shall have the regulation of such parts of the Capitol, and of its passages, as are or may be set apart for the use of the Senate and its officers. The Presiding Officer of the 48

SENATE. Restriction on presenting rejected claims to the. (See *Rule*)... 49

SENATE. Penalty of an officer or member for violating the confidence of the.................:.. 50

SENATE. The Senators and Secretary, before entering upon their duties, shall take and subscribe the oath prescribed by the act of July 2, 1862, in open 51

SENATORS of the United States. (See *Members*.)

SENSE of the Senate on any question of order. The President may call for the... 6

SERGEANT-AT-ARMS, or any other authorized person, may be sent for absent members. The... 8

SERGEANT-AT-ARMS and doorkeeper and assistant doorkeeper admitted in secret session. The....................................... 41

SESSION. Organization and commencement of business of each day's.... 1

SESSION, should less than a quorum appear, absent members may be sent for, &c. At the commencement or during any..................... 8

SESSION of the Senate, if the matter is in possession of the Senate. A motion for reconsideration may be made within two next days of actual.. 20

SHUT the doors, the gallery shall be cleared. On a motion made and seconded to 18

SPEAK shall address the Chair, stand at his place, and sit down when finished. Every member rising to................................. 3

SPEAK more than twice in one debate on same day without leave of the Senate. No member shall 4

SPEAK first; but the member rising and addressing the Chair first shall speak first. When two members rise, the President shall name the member to 5

SPEAKING to another member so as to interrupt business prohibited....... 2

SPEAKING in debate, no interruption to be made by talking, reading newspapers, or otherwise. While a member is.......................... 2

No.

SPEAKING or otherwise shall transgress the rules, he shall be called to order.
    If any member in...   6
SPECIAL orders of the day. The unfinished business at preceding adjourn-
    ment shall have preference in the................................   15
SPECIAL order, it shall be the duty of the Chair to take up such special
    order, and the Senate shall proceed to consider it, unless it be post-
    ·poned by vote of the Senate. When the hour shall have arrived for
    the consideration of a...   31
SPECIAL orders, according to the order of time *for* which they were assigned,
    and *at* which they were assigned, and over general orders, &c. Pre-
    cedence of..   31
SPECIAL orders shall not lose their positions on account of intervening ad-
    journments; nor shall they lose their relative position on the calendar,
    except by vote of the Senate, until finally disposed of.........   31
SPECIAL orders shall always have precedence of general orders, unless such
    special orders shall be postponed by direction of the Senate. When
    two or more subjects shall have been assigned for the same hour, the
    subject first assigned for that hour shall take precedence, but........   31
SPECIAL order not to be made without the concurrence of two-thirds present   31
SPECIALLY assigned for consideration, they shall take precedence according
    to the order of time *at* which they were severally assigned, and such
    order shall at no time be lost or changed, except by the direction of
    the Senate. When two or more subjects shall have been...........   31
STANDING committees of the Senate, shall not be referred to the Committee
    on Printing. Motions to print, by order of the.................   34
STANDING committees of the Senate shall be appointed at the commencement
    of each session, with leave to report by bill or otherwise, viz:
        On Foreign Relations, to consist of seven members.............   34
        On Finance, to consist of seven members.......................   34
        On Appropriations, to consist of seven members................   34
        On Commerce, to consist of seven members......................   34
        On Manufactures, to consist of five members...................   34
        On Agriculture, to consist of five members....................   34
        On Military Affairs and the Militia, to consist of seven members......   34
        On Naval Affairs, to consist of seven members.................   34
        On Judiciary, to consist of seven members.....................   34
        On Post Offices and Post Roads, to consist of seven members........   34
        On Public Lands, to consist of seven members..................   34
        On Private Land Claims, to consist of five members............   34
        On Indian Affairs, to consist of seven members................   34
        On Pensions, to consist of seven members......................   34
        On Revolutionary Claims, to consist of five members...........   34
        On Claims, to consist of seven members........................   34
        On District of Columbia, to consist of seven members.........   34
        On Patents and the Patent Office, to consist of five members.........   34
        On Public Buildings and Grounds, to consist of five members........   34

No.

On Territories, to consist of seven members 34
On the Pacific Railroad, to consist of nine members 34
On Mines and Mining, to consist of seven members 34
To Audit and Control the Contingent Fund, to consist of three members 34
On Printing, to consist of three members 34
On Engrossed Bills, to consist of three members 34
On Enrolled Bills, to consist of three members 34
STANDING committees, the Senate will proceed, by ballot, severally to appoint the chairman of each committee, and then, by one ballot, the other members necessary to complete the same; and a majority of the whole number of votes given shall be necessary to the choice of a chairman of a standing committee. All other committees shall be appointed by ballot, and a plurality of votes shall make a choice. In the appointment of the 35
STANDING committee shall first be put. When motions are made for reference of the same subject to a select committee and to a standing committee, the question on reference to the 36
STATES, not referred to the Committee on Printing. Motions to print documents from the legislatures or conventions lawfully called of the 34
STRIKE out and insert shall not be divided. A motion to 12
STRIKE out and insert one proposition shall not prevent a motion to strike out and insert a different proposition, nor a motion simply to strike out, nor shall the rejection of this prevent a motion to strike out and insert. A motion to 12
SUBJECT or matter shall have been referred to a committee, any other subject or matter of a similar nature may, on motion, be referred to such committee. When any 35
SUM first put. In filling blanks the largest 13
SUSPEND the 16th and 17th joint rules, &c., always in order, &c. A motion to 53
SUSPENSION or amendment of a rule. One day's notice to be given of a motion for the 53

T.

TABLE, and read before being debated. A motion made and seconded shall be reduced to writing, if desired, delivered in at the 10
TABLE, &c. (See Rule.) When a question is under debate no motion shall be received but to lie on the 11
TABLE. A brief statement of the contents of petitions, &c., to be made before being received or read at the 24
TABLE one day for consideration. All resolutions (not joint) and reports of committees shall lie on the 26
TERRITORIES, to consist of seven members. A standing Committee on ... 34
TIE vote of the Senate, the Secretary shall take the decision of the President. When there is a 21

No.

TIME, first put. In filling blanks the longest............................. 13

TITLES of bills, and parts affected by amendments, inserted on the journal. 32

TREATY, bill, or resolution, as in the Committee of the Whole, a chairman
    may be appointed by the Presiding Officer, &c. When the Senate shall
    consider a... 28

TREATIES. Proceedings on 38

TREATIES which may be laid before the Senate shall also be kept secret
    until the Senate shall, by their resolution, take off the injunction of
    secrecy. All.. 39

TREATIES, &c., shall be returned or delivered from the office of the Secre-
    tary without an order of the Senate for that purpose. No paper, ex-
    cept original 43

TWICE in any one debate. No member shall speak more than........... 4

TWO-THIRDS requisite to decide affirmatively on all amendments to treaties,
    and on the final question of ratification of treaties.................... 38

TWO-THIRDS shall not be requisite except on the final question. When an
    amendment to the Constitution is under consideration the concur-
    rence of............ 44

TWO-THIRDS of the members present are necessary to carry the affirmative,
    any member who votes on that side which prevailed in the question
    may be at liberty to move for a reconsideration ; and a motion for recon-
    sideration shall be decided by a majority of votes. When any question
    may have been decided by the Senate in which..................... 20

TWO-THIRDS present. No special order to be made without concurrence of. 31

U.

UNANIMOUS consent of the members present. On the third reading of any
    bill, &c., no amendment shall be received unless by the 29

UNANIMOUSLY direct otherwise. When nominations are made a future
    day shall be assigned for their consideration, unless the Senate 37

UNFINISHED business at preceding adjournment shall have preference in
    special orders of the day. The..................................... 15

V.

VERBAL statement of contents of a petition, &c., to be made before being
    received or read at the table. A brief............................... 24

VICE-PRESIDENT, or President of the Senate pro tem., shall have the right
    to name a member to perform the duties of the chair ; but such substi-
    tution shall not extend beyond an adjournment. The............... 23

VICE-PRESIDENT, or President pro tem., may call a member to fill the
    chair, &c. When the Senate shall consider a treaty, bill, or resolution
    in Committee of the Whole, the 28

VICE-PRESIDENT of the United States. (See *President of the Senate.*)

VOTE of the Senate, and without debate. When the reading of a paper is
    objected to it shall be determined by a 14

No.

VOTE, unless for special reasons he be excused. On every question taken
  by yeas and nays, each member shall 16

VOTE. When a decision is announced from the Chair no member shall be
  permitted to... 17

VOTE may be made before the subject has gone out of the possession of the
  Senate, if made same day or within two next days of actual session.
  On motion by one of the majority, the reconsideration of a........... 20

VOTE of the Senate, the Secrétary shall take the decision of the President.
  When there is a tie 21

VOTE of the Senate. Special orders shall have precedence over general
  orders unless postponed by a.. 31

VOTE of the Senate shall be entered on the journal. Every 33

VOTES given is necessary; and in appointment of all the committees, with
  that exception, a plurality of votes will make a choice. In the appointment of the chairman of standing committees a majority of all the..... 35

VOTES on amendments, &c., to treaties confirmed by the Senate shall be
  reduced to the form of a ratification, &c........................... 38

VOTES on that side which prevailed may move for a reconsideration, which
  shall be decided by a majority of votes. When two-thirds are requisite, any member who... 20

W.

WITHDRAWN by the mover before decision, amendment, or ordering of the
  yeas and nays, except a motion to reconsider, &c. Any motion may be 10

WITHDRAWN without leave of the Senate. A motion to *reconsider* shall
  not be.. 10

WORDS of a Senator called to order shall be taken down in writing, to
  enable the President to judge. The exceptionable................... 7

WRITING, &c. Exceptionable words in debate called to order shall be
  taken down in.. 7

WRITING, if desired by the President. A motion made and seconded shall
  be reduced to... 10

Y.

YEAS and nays are ordered, a motion cannot be withdrawn by the mover
  without leave of the Senate. When the................................ 10

YEAS and nays, and on a call of the house, the names of the members shall
  be taken alphabetically. In taking the............................ 16

YEAS and nays shall be called for by one-fifth of the Senators present, each
  shall answer, without debate, unless excused for special reason. When
  the 16

YEAS and nays are taken, no member shall vote after the decision is announced from the Chair. When the................................ 17

INDEX

TO

THE JOINT RULES OF THE TWO HOUSES OF CONGRESS.

A.

No.

ADDRESS to the President of the United States, it shall be presented to him in his audience chamber by the President of the Senate, in the presence of the Speaker and both houses. When the Senate and House of Representatives shall judge it proper to make a joint....... 11

ADHERED to their disagreement, a bill or resolution shall be lost. After each house shall have.. 15

AMENDMENTS between the Senate and House of Representatives. Regulations for conference on.. 1

B.

BILLS agreed to in one house and dissented to in the other, if either house shall request a conference and appoint a committee, and the other house shall also appoint a committee, they shall freely confer, &c. (See *Rule for proceedings*).. 1

BILLS are on their passage between the two houses, they shall be on paper, and under the signature of the Secretary or Clerk of each house, respectively. While.. 5

BILL shall have passed both houses, it shall be duly enrolled on parchment by the Clerk of the House of Representatives or Secretary of the Senate, as the bill may have originated in the one or the other house, before it shall be presented to the President of the United States. After a 6

BILLS are enrolled, they shall be examined by a joint committee of two from the Senate and two from the House of Representatives, appointed as a standing committee for that purpose, who shall carefully compare the enrollment with the engrossed bills, as passed in the two houses, and, correcting any errors that may be discovered in the enrolled bills, make their report forthwith to their respective houses. When... 7

BILL shall be signed in the respective houses, first by the Speaker of the House of Representatives, then by the President of the Senate. After examination and report, each....................................... 8

BILL shall have been thus signed in each house, it shall be presented by the said committee to the President of the United States for his appro-

6

No.

bation, (it being first indorsed on the back of the roll, certifying in
which house the same originated, which indorsement shall be signed
by the Secretary or Clerk, as the case may be, of the house in which
the same did originate,) and shall be entered on the journal of each
house. The said committee shall report the day of presentation to the
President, which time shall also be carefully entered on the journal
of each house. After a   9

BILLS. All orders, resolutions, and votes which are to be presented to the
President of the United States for his approbation shall also, in the
same manner, be previously enrolled, examined, and signed, and shall
be presented in the same manner and by the same committee as provided in the cases of bills   10

BILL or resolution which shall have passed in one house is rejected in the
other, notice thereof shall be given to the house in which the same
shall have passed. When a   12

BILL or resolution which has been passed in one house shall be rejected in
the other, it shall not be brought in during the same session without a
notice of ten days, and leave of two-thirds of that house in which it
shall be renewed. When a   13

BILL or resolution shall be founded. Each house shall transmit to the
other all papers on which any   14

BILL or resolution shall be lost. After each house shall have adhered to
their disagreement, a   15

BILL that shall have passed one house shall be sent for concurrence to the
other on either of the last three days of the session. No   16
    (For motion to suspend, see 26th Rule of Senate.)

BILL or resolution that shall have passed the House of Representatives and
the Senate shall be presented to the President of the United States for
his approbation on the last day of the session. No   17
    (For motion to suspend, see 26th Rule of Senate.)

BILLS which have passed one house are ordered to be printed in the other,
a greater number of copies shall not be printed than may be necessary
for the use of the house making the order. When   18

BILLS, resolutions, or reports which originated in either house, and at the
close of the next preceding session remain undetermined in either
house, shall be resumed and acted on in the same manner as if an
adjournment had not taken place. *After six days* from the commencement of a second or subsequent session of Congress, all   21

BUSINESS, consisting of bills, resolutions, or reports, which originated in
either house, and at the close of the next preceding session remained
undetermined in either house, shall be resumed and acted on in the
same manner as if an adjournment had not taken place. After six
days from the commencement of a second or subsequent session of
Congress, all (*Joint Rule*)   21

C.

CAPITOL, or on the public grounds adjacent thereto. No intoxicating liquors shall be offered for sale or exhibited within the...... 19

CEREMONIES and regulations in communicating messages between the two houses of Congress... 2

CLERK of the House of Representatives, respectively, shall sign all bills on paper between the two houses. The Secretary of the Senate and.. 5

CLERK of the House and Secretary of the Senate, respectively, shall enroll on parchment the bills as they may have originated in the one or the other house. The.. 6

CLERK of the House of Representatives, respectively, shall indorse on each enrolled bill in which house it originated. The Secretary of the Senate and... 9

COMMITTEES of conference on amendments to bills, &c., between the two houses. Regulations for joint...................................... 1

COMMITTEE of the two houses. Enrolled bills shall be examined by a joint 7

COMMITTEE on the Library, to consist of three members on the part of the Senate, and three on the part of the House of Representatives, to superintend and direct the expenditure of all moneys appropriated for the library, and to perform such other duties as are or may be directed by law. There shall be a joint..................................... 20

CONCURRENCE to the other on either of the three last days of the session. No bill that shall have passed one house shall be sent for............ 16

CONFERENCES on disagreeing votes on amendments to bills, &c., between the two houses. Regulations for................................. 1

CORRECT errors in enrolled bills. The joint committee may............. 7

D.

DISAGREEMENT a bill or resolution shall be lost. After each house shall have adhered to their... 15

DOORKEEPER of the House of Representatives shall announce messages from the Senate... 2

DOORKEEPER of the Senate shall announce messages from the House of Representatives, (Joint Rule)..................................... 3

E.

ELECTORAL votes for President and Vice-President. Regulating the proceedings of the two houses assembled in joint meeting for counting the 22

ENGROSSED on paper and signed by the Secretary or Clerk. Bills on paper between the two houses shall be.............................,... 5

ENROLLED on parchment by the Clerk of the House of Reprentatives, or the Secretary of the Senate, as the bill may have originated in the one or the other house, before it shall be presented to the President of the

No.

United States. After a bill shall have passed both houses it shall be
duly 6

ENROLLED, they shall be examined by a joint committee of two from the
Senate and two from the House of Representatives, appointed as a
standing committtee for that purpose, who shall carefully compare the
enrollment with the engrosed bills, as passed in the two houses, and,
correcting any errors that may be discovered in the enrolled bills, make
their report forthwith to their respective houses. When bills are.... 7

ENROLLED bill shall be signed in the respective houses, first by the Speaker
of the House of Representatives, then by the President of the Senate.
After examination and report, each................................... 8

ENROLLED bills after being signed by the Presiding Officer, shall be presented by the joint committee to the President of the United States
for his approbation, and, on their report, the time to be entered on the
journal 9

ENROLLED, examined, and signed, and shall be presented like bills. All
orders, resolutions, and votes which are to be presented to the President
of the United States for his approbation shall also, in the same manner,
be previously 10

ENROLLED bills not to be presented to the President the last day of the
session 17

ERRORS in enrolled bills. The joint committee may correct.............. 7

EXAMINED by a joint committee of the two houses. Enrolled bills &c.,
shall be... 7

G.

GROUNDS. No spirituous or malt liquors shall be sold in the Capitol or
adjacent public... 19

H.

HOUSE of Representatives to the Senate. Regulations and ceremonies
concerning messages from the..................................... 2

HOUSE may determine to be proper. Messages between the two houses
shall be sent by such persons as a sense of propriety in each......... 4

HOUSE. The Secretary of the Senate and Clerk of the House of Representatives shall enroll on parchment the bills as they may have originated
in the one or the other... 6

HOUSE in which the same shall have passed. When a bill or resolution
which shall have passed in one house is rejected in the other, notice
thereof shall be given to the....................................... 12

HOUSE shall be rejected in the other, it shall not be brought in during the
same session without a notice of ten days and leave of two-thirds of
that house in which it shall be renewed. When a bill or resolution
which has been passed in one...................................... 13

HOUSE shall transmit to the other all papers on which any bill or resolution
shall be founded. Each... 14

No

HOUSE shall have adhered to their disagreement, a bill or resolution shall
be lost. After each 15

HOUSE shall be sent for concurrence to the other on either of the three last
days of the session. No bill that shall have passed one.............. 16

HOUSES of Congress shall be presented to the President of the United
States for his approbation on the last day of the session. No bill or
resolution that shall have passed the two 17

HOUSE are ordered to be printed in the other, a greater number of copies
shall not be printed than may be necessary for the use of the house
making the order. When bills which have passed one.............. 18

HOUSE, and at the close of the next preceding session remained in either
house, shall be resumed and acted on in the same manner as if an
adjournment had not taken place. After six days from the commencement of a second or subsequent session of Congress, all bills,
resolutions, or reports, which originated in either.................... 21

HOUSES on the library. Appointment and duties of the joint committee of
the two.. 20

HOUSES of Congress. When the two Houses shall present a joint address
to the President, it shall be presented to him in his audience chamber
by the President of the Senate, in the presence of the Speaker and
both 11

I.

INTOXICATING liquors shall be offered for sale, or exhibited, within the
Capitol, or on the public grounds adjacent thereto. No 19

J.

JOINT committee of conference on amendments to bills between the two
houses. Regulations for.. 1

JOINT committee of the two houses. Enrolled bills shall be examined by a 7

JOINT committee to the President of the United States for his approbation,
and reported to the respective houses. Enrolled bills, after being
signed by the presiding officers, shall be presented by the............ 9

JOINT committee as provided in the cases of bills. All orders, resolutions,
and votes which are to be presented to the President of the United
States for his approbation, shall also be enrolled, examined, and signed,
and shall be presented in the same manner and by the same.......... 10

JOINT Committee on the Library, to consist of three members on the part of
the Senate and three on the part of the House of Representatives, to
superintend and direct the expenditure of all moneys appropriated for
the library, and to perform such other duties as are or may be directed
by law. There shall be a... 20

JOINT meeting of the two houses for counting the electoral votes for President and Vice-President. Regulating the proceedings in............. 22

No.

JOURNAL of each house. The examination, signing by the presiding officers, and presentation to the President of each enrolled bill, shall be
carefully entered upon the   9

L.

LEAVE of two-thirds of that house in which it shall be renewed. When
a bill or resolution which has been passed in one house shall be rejected
in the other, it shall not be brought in during the same session without
notice of ten days and 13
LIBRARY, to consist of three members on the part of the Senate and three
on the part of the House of Representatives, to superintend and direct
the expenditure of all moneys appropriated for the library, and to perform such other duties as are or may be directed by law. There shall
be a Joint Committee on the 20
LIQUORS shall be offered for sale or exhibited within the Capitol, or on the
public grounds adjacent thereto. No intoxicating 19

M.

MESSAGE shall be sent from the Senate to the House of Representatives,
it shall be announced at the door of the House by the Doorkeeper, and
shall be respectfully communicated to the Chair by the person by whom
it may be sent. When a   2
MESSAGE sent from the House of Representatives to the Senate...........   3
(Regulations and ceremonies same as above.)
MESSAGES between the two Houses shall be sent by such persons as a sense
of propriety in each house may determine to be proper...............   4

N.

NOTICE thereof shall be given to the house in which the same shall have
passed. When a bill or resolution which shall have passed in one
house is rejected in the other...................................... 12
NOTICE of ten days, and leave of two-thirds of that house in which it shall
be renewed. When a bill or resolution which has passed in one house
shall be rejected in the other, it shall not be brought in during the
same session without a 13

O.

ORDERS, resolutions, and votes which are to be presented to the President,
shall be enrolled, examined, signed, and presented like bills......... 10

P.

PAPERS on which any bill or resolution shall be founded. Each house
shall transmit to the other all.................................... 14

No.

PASSAGE between the two houses, they shall be on paper and under the
signature of the Secretary or Clerk of each house, respectively. While
bills are on their.. 5

PRESENTED to the President of the United States by the joint committee
for his approbation, (being first indorsed on the back of the roll by
the Secretary or Clerk certifying in which house it originated,) the
presentation to be entered on the journal, when the committee shall
report the day of presentation to the President. After an enrolled bill
shall be signed it shall be... 9

PRESENTED to the President shall be enrolled, signed, and presented like
bills. All orders, resolutions, and votes which are to be.............. 10

PRESENTED to him in his audience chamber by the President of the Senate,
in the presence of the Speaker and both houses. When the Senate and
House of Representatives shall judge it proper to make a joint address
to the President of the United States, it shall be.................... 11

PRESIDENT of the Senate. After examination and report, each enrolled bill
shall be signed by the Speaker of the House of Representatives and... 8

PRESIDENT of the Senate, in the presence of the Speaker and both houses.
When the Senate and House of Representatives make a joint address
to the President, it shall be presented to him in his audience chamber
by the.. 11

PRESIDENT of the United States. Bills passed by both houses shall be
enrolled on parchment, &c., before they shall be presented to the..... 6

PRESIDENT of the United States for his approbation. Enrolled bills, after
being signed, &c., shall be presented by the joint committee to the.... 9

PRESIDENT of the United States shall be enrolled, signed, and presented
like bills. All orders, resolutions, and votes which are to be presented
to the 10

PRESIDENT of the United States, it shall be presented to him in his audience
chamber by the President of the Senate, in the presence of the Speaker
and both houses. When the Senate and House of Representatives shall
judge it proper to make a joint address to the 11

PRESIDENT of the United States for his approbation on the last day of the
session. No bill or resolution that shall have passed the two houses
shall be presented to the... 17

PRESIDENT and Vice-President. Regulating the proceedings of the two
houses assembled in joint meeting for counting the electoral votes for.. 22

PRINTED in the other, a greater number of copies shall not be printed than
may be necessary for the use of the house making the order. When
bills which have passed one house are ordered to be.................. 18

PUBLIC grounds adjacent thereto. No intoxicating liquors shall be offered
for sale or exhibited within the Capitol, or on the 19

R.

REJECTED in the other, notice thereof shall be given to the house in which
the same shall have passed. When a bill or resolution which shall
have passed in one house is... 12

No.

REJECTED in the other, it shall not be brought in during the same session without notice of ten days, and leave of two-thirds of that house in which it shall be renewed. When a bill or resolution which has been passed in one house shall be 13

REPORT to the respective houses. The Joint Committee on Enrolled Bills shall, after examination, forthwith.................................. 7

REPORTS originating in either house, and undisposed of at the end of the next preceding session, shall be resumed and acted on, after six days from the commencement of a second or subsequent session, in same manner as if an adjournment had not taken place.................... 21

RESOLUTIONS, &c., which are to be presented to the President shall be enrolled, examined, and signed, and presented like bills............. 10

RESOLUTIONS originating in either house, and undisposed of at the end of the next preceding session, shall be resumed and acted on, after six days from the commencement of a second or subsequent session, in same manner as if an adjournment had not taken place............... 21

S.

SECRETARY of the Senate and Clerk of the House of Representatives, respectively, shall sign all (engrossed) bills on passage between the two houses. The 5

SECRETARY of the Senate and Clerk of the House of Representatives, respectively, shall enroll on parchment the bills as they may have originated in the one or the other house, &c. The....................... 6

SECRETARY of the Senate and Clerk of the House of Representatives, respectively, shall indorse on each enrolled bill in which house it originated 9

SENATE to the House of Representatives. Regulations and ceremonies for messages from the 2, 3

SENATE and House of Representatives shall judge it proper to make a joint address to the President, it shall be presented to him in his audience chamber by the President of the Senate, in the presence of the Speaker and both houses. When the....................................... 11

SESSION. No bill that shall have passed one house shall be sent for concurrence to the other on either of the three last days of the........... 16

SESSION. No bill or resolution that shall have passed the two houses shall be presented to the President of the United States for his approbation on the last day of the... 17

SIGNED by the Speaker of the House of Representatives and President of the Senate. After examination and report, each enrolled bill shall be. 8

SPEAKER of the House of Representatives and President of the Senate. After examination and report, each enrolled bill shall be signed by the. 8

SPIRITS prohibited in the Capitol or Capitol grounds. Intoxicating...... 19

T.

TWO-THIRDS of that house in which it shall be renewed. When a bill or

No.

resolution which has been passed in one house shall be rejected in the
other, it shall not be brought in during the same session without notice
of ten days and leave of... 13

U.

UNFINISHED business at the close of a first session of Congress, which
originated in either house, &c., shall be resumed, after six days from
the commencement of a second or subsequent session, in the same
manner as if an adjournment had not taken place. The............. 21

V.

VICE-PRESIDENT. Regulating the proceedings of the two houses assembled
in joint meeting for counting the electoral votes for President and..... 22
VOTES, resolutions, and orders which are to be presented to the President
shall be enrolled, signed, and presented like bills................... 10
VOTES for President and Vice-President. Regulating the proceedings of the
two houses assembled in joint meeting for counting the electoral...... 22

7

CPSIA information can be obtained
at www.ICGtesting.com
Printed in the USA
BVOW06*1316180117

473854BV00004B/14/P

9 781356 833450